The Messy Truth

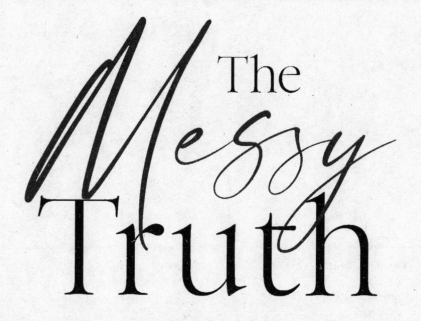

The Messy Truth

How I Sold My Business for Millions
but Almost Lost Myself

Alli Webb

HARPER HORIZON

ISBN 978-1-4003-3374-5 (eBook)
ISBN 978-1-4003-3373-8 (HC)

Library of Congress Control Number: 2023938550

Printed in the United States of America
23 24 25 26 27 LBC 5 4 3 2 1

To my light and joy, Grant and Kit, for your
unconditional love, support, and honesty.
My gratitude and appreciation for you is endless.

Contents

Part 1: What a Mess

1. I'm Not Your Average Entrepreneur   3
2. Balance Is Bullshit   19
3. It Just Happened   37
4. The Truth About Overnight Success   59

Part 2: Your Mess Is Your Magic

5. When Business Booms, Someone's Getting Divorced   81
6. This May Surprise You   101
7. The Rise and Fall of a Great Idea   119

Part 3: Embrace Your Mess

8. The Hardest Job of All   137
9. When Life Gives You Lemons, Go Buy Some Fucking Limes   159
10. Your Great Big Idea Is Usually Your Next One   177
11. You're Going to Be Fine . . . Mostly   193

Afterword   207
Acknowledgments   211
Notes   213
About the Author   215

Part One

What a Mess

Chapter One

I'm Not Your Average Entrepreneur

You can be raw, real, and messy and still
build a successful career and life.

*H*ow did I get here?

I'm sitting in my Spanish-meets-Craftsman California home with my new husband and numerous exciting ventures underway. We have a happily blended family, a cat named Cookie, and time to spend on work and play. (I just got back from a spa weekend in Palm Springs. I'm hydrated, moisturized, and loved! Yay!)

To the outside world, I've got it all: I'm a successful entrepreneur, and I have a beautiful family, a lovely home, and a lot of really exciting projects on the horizon.

That's what we all want, right?

Oh, please.

You don't really believe that.

Do you? Ask yourself: *Is what Alli has what I really want?* Is what so-and-so posts to the Gram really what's important to you? Do you *really* want to waste "your one wild and precious life" (thanks, Mary Oliver[1]) scrolling, hearting, and commenting on someone else's success? Or do you want to go out and build your own?

If that's you—if you're really committed to this—here's the catch: to build your own business you have to understand the struggles, the setbacks, the pain, and the potential failure.

Basically, you have to get up close and personal with some *deep, dark shit.*

Meaning: if you've come to this book for fluffy takeaways on how to reach millionaire status, this isn't for you (though I will tell you how I sold my company for millions). If you've come to this book to read a sugarcoated, generic success story, I'm afraid you're going to be really disappointed. Though I *have* had success, it hasn't always been pretty—in fact, as you might guess from the title, it's had its fair share of messiness. As so many people know, the more your stock rises professionally, the more your personal life implodes.

I am a living, breathing example of just how high one can climb and how fast one can fall. But no one wants to celebrate that, do they? They want the cover of *Inc.* magazine, the guest appearances on *Shark Tank*, the accolades and accomplishments. I get it. I want all that too.

Most people want the success story, not the messy truth.

Don't get me wrong: I want you to build your big business. I want you to have your fluffy cat and your hot partner. I want you to find love and money. I want you to have it all.

But I don't want you to do it by living someone else's story. I want you to *own your shit.*

I want you to embrace your mess.

I want you to find the magic in your chaos.

I want you to be real.

. . . .

While you probably know me best from Drybar, the nation's premier blow-dry bar, specializing in only blowouts—no cuts, no color—there's a *lot* more to my story than that. Yes, to date, there are over 150 Drybar locations and over four thousand employees. And yes, in 2020, Drybar was acquired for over $255 million. (And no, I did not walk away with that amount in my pocket.)

When we launched in 2010, my cofounders were my now ex-husband, Cameron Webb (the genius behind the brand), and my brother Michael Landau (the business brain who helped make my dream a reality. Thanks, bro).

Before we started Drybar in 2008, I never thought much about being an entrepreneur. I did start a dog-walking business (not my best idea) and my parents were entrepreneurs, but I didn't get the business bug until I dreamed up Drybar after an aha moment of realizing there was an unfulfilled need out there—a need I personally felt I could fulfill. I'd spent many years struggling with my naturally curly and frizzy hair, so I knew what the power of a blowout could do—how it could transform someone's self-confidence. Because of my own hair, I learned to love blowouts, especially when I began working in salons.

Necessity is the mother of invention, after all. (Thanks, Plato.[2] You really knew your shit.) I had pretty good instincts. But in terms of building an empire? Well, that wasn't top of mind.

What *was* top of mind was finding something I was passionate about—but on my own terms. I was searching for purpose, something just for me. I wasn't looking to make a million dollars; instead, I was on a quest for happiness, which I think has always been a guiding light of mine. This was before the social media bonanza and before FOMO was a thing. I was a pretty run-of-the-mill mama who went to the park one too many times during the week and realized it was time to get back a little bit of me. When I decided to focus on reclaiming my own identity, a few key pieces fell into place.

. . . .

Though entrepreneurs today face different challenges (more noise, more competition, etc.), it still always starts with *you*: *your* idea, *your* skill set, *your* purpose, and *your* gut instinct. What is that thing you just can't stop thinking about?

I knew from the start that I wanted to build something I sincerely loved that brought me joy and served women. I wanted people I trusted around me. I wanted family.

I wasn't entirely certain what type of leader I would be (I definitely wasn't asking myself questions like that back then!), but I did know the skills and passions I brought to the table. I wanted to lead with kindness, inclusivity, and the attitude of "no job is too small or tedious for the ultimate boss." But back in 2010, there weren't as many readily available stories of respected entrepreneurs as there are today. It was a very different time. As a result, I felt pretty alone in trying to figure it out.

I was as scrappy as they come. I'd honed my skill sets in so many hair salons over the years that I knew what it was like to be on *all* sides of the salon business, not just out front. (This would become a huge asset to me later—stay tuned.)

Because I wasn't in a rush to build a giant empire—I never even thought about it, actually—I was able to start small (more on that later) and grow organically. I wasn't obsessed with reaching millions immediately (I didn't think about that stuff at all back then); instead, I was focused on finding my personal purpose and providing the absolute *best* experience to women. Period.

That's what mattered most to me: that women walked away feeling better about themselves. I learned that making people feel good made *me* feel good. Win-fucking-win.

During those first few years, as we built Drybar, it seemed

like a fairy tale. I scaled the blockbuster brand with my two favorite men. I was being seen, validated, and rewarded for the work I'd done. I had figured it out! And I was getting noticed and accoladed by an adoring public, which is what we all want, right?

Like most women who do too much, I appeared calm to that same adoring public, but really, I was like a duck, paddling my feet like mad beneath the water's surface. I had to fight to keep up appearances: a happy marriage, two amazing kids, a thriving business, a perfect life! But the reality was that I was struggling internally. While my external life was a frenzy of activity, nothing paralleled the noise of my internal struggles.

I would tell myself that my husband and I were happy enough. Who cared if we didn't have regular sex or intimacy? Lust was *supposed* to wear off over time, right? Who cared if I was purposely distracting myself from my emotions by burying myself in work and shopping excessively? I had a killer business and a brand, two healthy boys, and I was living the American dream.

I had it all, dammit!

I swept all the other shit far under the rug, went to therapy (couples therapy too), but mostly I succumbed to the temptation of instant gratification. Yup, I shopped. I felt better. I felt worse. I shopped some more, searching for that instant dopamine rush. I was a shit show, but I couldn't see it yet.

I wouldn't see that truth for a very long time.

My need for distraction was bigger than just overspending on clothes, bags, and shoes. I was also addicted to moving—we would upgrade to a new house every two years or so, which meant my sons never established good friend groups, and as a result, I think they often felt isolated (which I totally regret).

But I couldn't help myself. I'm a fast mover, always have been. I'm incredibly decisive, which has been a blessing and a curse all rolled into one. It was like I needed a project, something new and shiny to keep me from thinking about what was really happening around me or how I was feeling about my life outside of work. I wasn't settled emotionally, and that manifested itself every time I physically uprooted my family. I assumed that a new start or new things would lead to a happier marriage and a more balanced life.

I know *now* that I was searching for a feeling of home, of intimacy (something I had never really experienced)—a feeling I did not get in my marriage. For a long time, I refused to entertain the idea of getting divorced because I had a picture in my head about who a divorced woman was, and I didn't want to be her. (I know, I know. Shame on me.) I didn't want to be divorced because I assumed that meant I'd failed or given up, so I desperately clung to the notion of keeping my vows and making it work.

Because who would I be if I wasn't married anymore?

At that time, I was too scared to find out. I'd wrapped my identity tightly around being the founder of Drybar. I liked my image of having it all: the business, the cool creative husband, and the cute sons with great hair. My image was exactly what I wanted it to be. Unfortunately, this grandiose image had so many holes, it looked like a piece of Swiss cheese.

After I sold my business (which we will also get to), the idea of starting my life over in my forties would require an understanding about how I had become the person who started Drybar, and why, for years, I stubbornly clung to the story I told myself about how my life was *supposed* to be.

I didn't want to break up my family. I didn't want to start over. I'd worked so hard, for so long, that the idea of beginning again felt insurmountable.

But then something happened in my life that forced me to wake up to the fact that I wasn't really happy, I wasn't thriving, and I wasn't being honest with myself. I couldn't keep up the facade any longer. It was a combination of things, really. In a nutshell, it was being exposed to a different kind of man; losing my mother; a bit of "oh shit, half my life is over so I better not waste any more time"; and craving a reinvention I didn't even know was waiting for me.

Suddenly, I couldn't leave my emotions unsettled. I couldn't *pretend* anymore.

I was going to have to face both myself and everything that I'd built before I blew it all up—one messy layer at a time.

Lessons I've Learned

The Sooner You Can Admit What's Swimming Beneath the Surface, the Sooner You Can Improve Your Life

This is not an easy task.

Getting real with yourself requires you to figure out what is lurking beneath the surface. For me, I realized I was conflict avoidant. I hated conflict, so I avoided it.

In the early days of Drybar, I would vent to my brother and let the resentment roll. You know what I'm talking about, right? You get frustrated at a team member, but you don't face it directly. Instead, you make passive-aggressive, snarky remarks about the situation or avoid dealing with that person and hold a grudge.

I realized this behavior was an attempt to gain control. As most of us know, we have very little control over very few things. The sooner we can give up our desire for control, the much better we will be. By the time I finally dealt with a lot of these situations, the damage was already done.

I was also guilty of wanting people to come to me to fix a problem and not the other way around. It's like when you're five and get into a fight with your sibling, and neither one of you wants to admit any wrongdoing.

What I now realize is that I sorely needed vulnerability. I missed this a lot back then (hell, I still miss it a lot now). But it's an important lesson and reminder nonetheless.

If there is internal conflict (at work, home, in the bedroom, etc.), chances are it's rubbing off on your entire orbit. It takes a lot of courage to jump in and deal with it. My best advice on the other side? Rip off the Band-Aid and get in there and see what happens.

You might be pleasantly surprised.

Own Who You Are Instead of Pretending to Be Someone Else

This is a tough one (catching a theme here?).

As an entrepreneur, you will be faced with tons of challenges and decision-making like never before. While I certainly believe in learning from those we admire, it's important—in fact, essential—to work toward becoming the absolute best version of *you*.

Finding your unique leadership style takes time to perfect. (Who am I kidding? It's never going to be perfect, but you can damn sure try!) It's a lot of trial and error. I used to lose my shit pretty easily when I walked into a Drybar shop, and it felt like major sensory overload. All I noticed was what was *wrong*—so much so that I often missed what was right. And while I strongly believe someone has to have a discerning eye, I had to learn a better, more productive way of giving feedback.

I'm a pretty reactive person by nature, so it's hard for me not to wear my emotions proudly on my sleeve for everyone to see.

But I learned over time, and during a lot of heartfelt conversations with my brother and John Hefner (Drybar CEO at the time), that I was doing more harm than good by essentially throwing a fit and making everyone uncomfortable.

I think a little discomfort is a good thing, but finding a balance is key. Over time, had my negative behavior continued, it would have been really detrimental to the business.

So what's the answer here? Be true to your best self; be honest with what's going on for you and what you want, and fit that into the version of yourself that brings out the best in others. Pursue feedback and have enough self-awareness to grow into a really kick-ass leader.

If You Feel Like an Imposter, Embrace It!

FOMO is real, y'all.

We *all* experience it. There's always going to be someone doing something or being someone you aspire to be. *Always.* So use that as motivation to work harder, shake things up, and begin creating the very thing you were envious of in the first place.

And while we are on the subject of comparing ourselves to others, let's talk about a term that gets a lot of attention: imposter syndrome, which is a fancy way of saying, "I feel insecure." It's like comparing our inside world to what we think we should be feeling like and looking like to others. Huh?

While imposter syndrome is often touted as something negative, it's quite positive if you really think about it. As leaders, we are taking risks daily and constantly stepping into roles we have not ventured into before.

So yes, when I decided to start and run my own company, I felt like a *total* imposter. Know why? Because I was! I was stepping into a role that was new to me. With a leap like that comes

13

a lot of experimentation plus loads of new responsibilities, which means tons of opportunities to fall flat on our faces and look silly or stupid or like we don't know what we're doing. So what? Being an entrepreneur is all about risk: putting yourself out there, taking chances, and figuring out how to make it all work. Trust me, it takes time and patience, so cut yourself some slack and have fun with it.

The moral of the story here is this: go fucking embrace the feeling of being an imposter! It might mean you're exactly where you're supposed to be.

Stop comparing
yourself to every other
entrepreneur and
trust your gut.

What are you not willing to talk about?

Chapter Two

Balance Is Bullshit

No one starts a successful business. You start a business and make it successful.

I've just got to find some balance."

Raise your hand if you've heard this common refrain.

Surely by now I'm not bursting anyone's Zen bubble when I remind you what you already know: *Balance is bullshit.* It's not real. Moreover, it's not even worth pursuing. (You're welcome—I just saved you a ton of time.)

And it's not just because we live in a go-go-go society, where hustle culture can feel as common as touching your phone twenty-six hundred times per day (yes, this is a real number—be very, very afraid).

If you want to build something big and fast, you have to be nimble, and there's not often ample time for rest, reflection, or midday yoga. If you're searching for a predictable schedule, I'm sorry to say the entrepreneur life isn't for you.

If you're just starting your entrepreneurial journey, it's important—*before you start*—to think through what type of culture you want to create and what pace you want to set. Are you a high-energy person? Are you organized? Do you lead by example?

. . . .

A huge mistake I made early in my entrepreneurial career was thinking I had to handle everything myself. I took the concept of micromanaging to a new level, and I suffered because of it.

When you're starting something new, it's easy to forget that you can't do everything if you want to grow. Ask for help!

No matter how much you think you can do everything by yourself, you really can't. You simply can't do it all—not well anyway.

This proved to be my Achilles' heel time and time again. My brother warned me. My ex-husband reminded me. My employees told me. But I had a vision, and I wanted to make sure that vision was upheld.

I was particular! I had standards! And, if I'm being honest, I was scared of someone else messing up what I'd built. I had a dream, and I wanted to see it through *my* way. But when you grip too tightly to something, when you are overly attached, it can potentially cause a lot of damage in the long run.

But doing things myself, *my way*, was always part of my attitude. From a very young age, when I worked in my parents' clothing store, Flip's, I realized that I simply didn't subscribe to doing things like everyone else. I knew what I liked and what I didn't like. I knew that my parents were giving me room to figure out what I wanted to do with my life and that my path didn't have to look like my brother's (back in the day, he could have given Alex P. Keaton from *Family Ties* a run for his money). I was taught to be a free thinker and to embrace my decisiveness, so while I struggled to find my professional path, I instinctively knew it would all work out.

Though I knew I didn't have to run myself into the ground, I realized quickly that I *liked* being busy. I *liked* juggling a lot. I *liked* the buzz of a sale. I *liked* being in the thick of things, especially when I started working in hair salons. I thrived in controlled chaos. I still do.

Once we began to build Drybar, I found that when I was truly passionate about something, I didn't mind spending all my time on it. The business also served as an excellent distraction from the things I *didn't* want to spend time on, like my flailing marriage.

When you're married and have kids, things can get super tricky as an entrepreneur. How is it possible to build a successful business (possibly with your spouse) and raise babies *at the same exact time*? To tend to your spouse *and* your kids *and* your bottom line *and* yourself? Pfft, good luck.

For me, it simply wasn't possible. I had to choose, and I had to choose often. This or that. Here or there. Him or me. All in or all out. Time flew, and as I grew more successful, my marriage's cracks started to show. Or at least that was what I told myself.

Pre-Drybar, I had spent the first five years at home with our boys while Cam built his impressive career in the advertising world. Almost overnight, our roles flipped.

I wasn't prepared for how quickly Drybar would grow, and I was even less prepared for the impact it would have on my personal life. To the public, I was killing it—but at home, the only thing I was killing was my marriage.

I met my ex-husband Cameron in Hell.

Hell was the name of a bar owned by some friends. It was situated smack in the middle of what is now the very trendy Meatpacking District in New York. I clocked a lot of hours in Hell.

The night I met Cameron, I stomped across the sticky floors, ordered a drink, and looked over all the beautiful gay men, crossing them off in my mind one by one. Then, after a few drinks, my friend Henry waved to get my attention across the packed bar.

He pointed to a guy and mouthed, "He's straight."

I rolled my eyes but assessed the guy in question. He was definitely cute and a dead ringer for Justin Timberlake. Curly hair spilled from underneath a ball cap, and his fitted short-sleeve button-down suggested the body of an endurance athlete. Henry was across the room, so the stranger and I introduced ourselves. All I said was "Hi," and this guy locked eyes with me and said, "You're the most beautiful girl I've ever seen."

He immediately flushed the shade of a beet. Embarrassed, he broke eye contact. "I can't believe I just said that," he muttered.

But that only drew me in further. He wasn't trying to flatter me into going home with him; he was being adorably sincere. Rather than writing him off as cheesy, I knew something genuine lurked behind his words. His honesty was refreshing.

"Want to hang out?" I asked.

He glanced at me, his mouth curling into a grin. "Definitely," he said.

From that first night together in Hell, Cam and I embarked on a hot and heavy romance that revolved around drugs, sex, and partying. (See? No balance in sight.) We were on cloud nine, having the time of our lives. It felt perfect. I was in my early twenties, and even while under the influence, I thought I'd found my person (and trust me, I was on the hunt!).

We had so much fun together. He liked to go out. I liked to go out. We both really liked to party, and most nights, we were out well past five in the morning but could still responsibly show up for our jobs. We were wildly attracted to each other. Plus, he was a creative at an ad agency, and those New York finance guys just didn't do it for me. He had a really cool job that was interesting and stable—a rare combination. He was The Guy. I just knew it.

Basically, in my twenty-something brain, Cam checked all the boxes.

After six months of dating, we went to visit his parents. I thought for sure he was going to propose because we were so in love. I knew he was The One, so really, I thought there was no need to wait any longer.

Welcome to my impatient side.

Though he did not propose on my timeline, our partying began to taper after those first six months, and so did our crazy sex life. I had experienced a drop-off in physical intimacy in all my previous relationships, so I wasn't concerned. It just seemed natural not to want to jump each other every five minutes, but gradually, problems began popping up left and right.

When the partying stopped and the drugs wore off, I got a clear picture of just how much Cam drank and how little I did. I would be half a glass of wine in, and Cam would be three or four beers deep. Yet, even while drinking, he was always kind and funny, and it was easier to sweep what felt like a habit (that would eventually grow to be a major problem) under the rug, rather than bring it up.

Even at such a young age, I felt I had too much to lose.

I tiptoed around this subject, because I wasn't going to fuck up the only equation that made sense in my brain: *man + marriage + babies = success.*

(I know, I know. Please hold the judgment.)

I decided to stay the course even though Cam's drinking really bothered me. I wanted to get married. I wanted the whole big, happy picture, and I constantly reminded myself that nobody was perfect. Who cared if he drank a lot?

Exactly one year after we met, on a hot summer day, Cam left me a hand-drawn map of Central Park, marked with an X on the exact spot I was to meet him. When I was running late, and, in typical Alli fashion, got lost and called him, confused, he sounded a little impatient. So I started to think that something must be up.

When I finally made it to the spot (sweating by this point, of course), he greeted me with a smile. I was reminded of all we'd been through in such a short time and that I wanted to share my life with this man.

I reached into the picnic basket he'd packed to grab a bottle of water when, all of a sudden, out popped the sweetest little puppy you've ever seen, wearing a Tiffany chain around its neck with a heart charm dangling from it. On it, the words "Will You Marry Me" were engraved.

I was giddy and crying. Strangers were clapping all around us.

Despite the warning bells chiming in my head—*Should we be having this many problems only a year into our relationship? Should I bring up the drinking? Should I bring up the fact that we're no longer having regular sex?*—I was all in. I decided to fill my head with happier thoughts—*I'm engaged! I have a fucking puppy! He went to Tiffany! I get to have what I always wanted!*

We forged on. It was all happening. My whole life, I'd been searching for what I wanted to do professionally and to have someone I loved to share it with. Now, here was a guy who wasn't perfect but pretty damn close, and I wasn't going to ruin it by worrying.

However, about a month before the wedding, while Cam and I were on a run (working on our wedding bods) in Washington Square Park, he stopped and said, "I'm worried about us getting married."

I stopped running, too, sure I hadn't heard him right. Of course, we couldn't call off the wedding *now*. Panic swirled, and my heart started beating erratically as I looked at him. "Why?" I finally responded. I thought about all the money we'd spent, all the people we'd invited, all the opinions and gossip that would erupt if we broke off our engagement. No thank you.

But deep, deep down (okay, not that deep), I knew he was right. Our foundation was shaky at best, but I didn't have enough self-awareness or courage to stop and really listen to what he was saying and what we were both feeling. We were best friends, and really enjoyed each other's company; wasn't that enough?

Instead of digging deeper into that statement, I talked him out of it. The wedding was set. We were walking down that aisle regardless, dammit.

As we got closer to the wedding, we swept our issues under the rug, along with everything else. After we got married, I entered a slew of jobs that were leading me closer and closer to hair—and then I finally got pregnant. We moved to Los Angeles and had our two boys. Mission accomplished.

. . . .

When I stumbled upon the idea that would ultimately become Drybar, I was mostly happy. *Mostly* happy in my marriage.

Mostly trying to find my way. *Mostly* focused on raising our two sons, Grant and Kit, who felt like the true loves of my life.

But I was also losing myself and what little balance I thought I'd claimed.

I was slipping into mom mode, and my fingers itched to build something, to find a purpose and passion outside of motherhood. I had spent hours upon hours at parks and mommy groups, music classes, the gym, play dates, breastfeeding support groups—you name it—during the first few years of being a mom, and I loved it for a while. But over time, the allure wore off and I found myself daydreaming of something just for me. All my fellow mamas out there know all too well that motherhood, while being one of the greatest gifts, is a selfless and thankless job.

I stumbled around again. Now in my midthirties, I had to figure out what lit me up. Who was I now besides Grant and Kit's mom and Cam's wife? I was searching and exploring. It was all I could think about at the time. What did I want to do next?

I'd spent time in New York searching for the right career. I'd worked for legendary hair stylist John Sahag. I'd worked for (late '90's) fashion icons like Cynthia Rowley and Nicole Miller. And I even moved back to Florida to open a Nicole Miller store with my brother that almost ruined our relationship. I went to hair school. I worked in salons. I started a dog-walking business, and then I decided to go into event planning with my best friend, Paige. Always seeking and searching!

I kept circling around what I *really* wanted to be doing, though I was finally dipping my toe into entrepreneurial waters. I was itching to do something, to build something, and I kept thinking back to my parents' clothing store, Flip's. I'd watched them build and grow and scale and not kill each other in the process.

I wanted to do something like that but make it my own.

I was unsure if I would ever find the thing that fit, the career that would drive me, or the business that would successfully combine my passions with lucrative work. I had discovered, after my experience marketing my event-planning business with Paige, that I was someone who craved connection. While Paige and I tried to make our event-planning business work, it just wasn't the right thing for me, and we both knew it.

I'll never forget the day, the very moment, when Paige and I were hanging out in my tiny, two-bedroom apartment in Santa Monica with our babies crawling around, and I got the courage to tell Paige I felt like I needed to pursue something I knew better and loved more than party planning: hair.

I had always loved doing blowouts. Back when I worked in a salon, I loved getting through a haircut just so I could get to the blowout, which was where you could see the results of the haircut and see it come to life, not to mention see a woman light up with delight. I missed that and needed to figure out how to get that feeling—while operating at my "new mom" pace.

I said to Paige, "I really miss doing hair and feel like it could be cool to start a mobile blowout business where I could go to the homes of new moms and blow out their hair while their babies are sleeping."

That idea came swift and fast, like most good things. Suddenly, I just *knew* what I wanted to do. I couldn't wipe the smile off my face.

I wanted to give women the same feeling I had when I walked out of a salon when I was a teenager. I wanted to make them feel confident and triumphant like I had felt after controlling my untamable hair, something that might seem insignificant but truly affected how I felt about myself. I wanted to provide an opportunity to sit down one-on-one with the people I worked for and give them a service tailored to their desires.

Just like that, I knew exactly what I wanted to do.

I wanted to start a blowout business for women.

Lessons I've Learned

If You Have an Idea That Won't Leave You Alone, See Where It Leads

Most of us have come up with a good idea or two in our lifetimes.

We get inspired. We want to go all in on something, but then life gets in the way, the idea fizzles, and we return to our comfort zones, right? I've been there, coming up with idea after idea, but I never seemed to follow through.

With my blowout business, it was different. It's something I truly and deeply loved, it was something I knew, and it was solving a problem. The idea seemed simple, not grandiose, and I knew that women would love it. It was fulfilling a need we all had: wanting our hair to look good.

When that idea latched on, I just couldn't shake it off. Ask yourself if you've ever had an idea like that. Is there something you can do, or have thought about doing, that keeps you up at night?

Take time to think it through. Talk about it. Dream about it. Then take action.

You never know where it might lead you.

When You Go All In, Boundaries Are the First Thing to Go

Balance really is an illusion.

I've never met a new entrepreneur (or parent) who is approaching this new phase of life with perfect balance and harmony. When growing anything—a partnership or a relationship—you sometimes approach it with obsessive attention. You live, breathe, eat, and sleep said idea or new paramour, because that's how you want to spend your time.

So what's wrong with that?

For most of us, nothing. However, in today's hyperconnected, reactive world, it's harder to maintain boundaries (which is even more important than balance). If your employees can reach you twenty-four hours a day, if you're sleeping with your phone by your head, if you're responding to emails at all hours, then trust me: you will eventually burn out.

While we can all work hard and approach our new idea with excitement, we must also take time to rest and process. I've come up with some of my best ideas when I've stepped away from both the phone and the business and just let my mind wander for a while.

Create healthy boundaries around work and pick a few activities that bring you joy. Do them regularly to bring a sense of balance and peace.

There Is No Timeline for Success: Forge Your Own Path

In today's world, it's easy to get ahead of ourselves.

We have an idea for a business, and we find someone on Instagram who has already built what we want to build. We're thinking about growing our business to seven figures before we've even gotten off the ground. We want to get some press hits and compare ourselves to entrepreneurs who have been on the cover of every magazine. It can feel like we are constantly behind or that everything we do seems pointless in the rat race.

Here's something to remember: this is *your* journey, not anyone else's. It's easy to get caught up in what everyone else is doing because it's all so accessible. Scrolling through the highlight reels, the constant accomplishments and accolades can make you feel like all you're chasing is the prize, not the journey.

If I've learned anything on this journey, it's that the big wins are fleeting. If you don't love what you do, then you most certainly won't be satisfied by the highs. You have to go into your journey with laser focus on what you want to build and what your goals are, and you need to know that no amount of money or success will ever change how fundamentally happy you are.

Build a solid foundation first, so the wins can just be icing on the cake.

You're not going to have
all the answers—
and that's okay.

What is your biggest fear?

Chapter Three

It Just Happened

Sometimes your best idea will come from
what you were passionate about as a child.

I think people would really love this, Al."

I was sitting on the living room floor, tending to my babies, when Paige uttered those words. I wasn't sure if she was serious.

The truth was, I had always been drawn to hair. When my hair was blown stick straight as a kid—way before I could appreciate it—I would fuss with it, gather it up and then let it spill down, and pile it into clips, barrettes, and my mom's personal favorite: pigtails. In a tragic turn of events, I got an ill-advised bowl cut because my childhood best friend, Cory, had one. I thought it was so cool. (For the record, bowl cuts are not cool, were never cool, and will never be cool—unless you're a Beatle, I guess?)

As a child of the 1970s, I fell under the impression that *tamable* hair equated to beauty. The hair that ruled the world at that time was big, bouncy, smooth waves. Everywhere I looked on TV or in magazines (before social media), models stared back at me with their shiny, soft, luscious locks, and I would think, *How in the world does their hair look like that? And why doesn't mine? And how do I get it?*

When my family moved to Florida, my hair got real frizzy real fast, and I would beg my mom to blow it straight. She did her best, but I was never satisfied and would complain it was still "bumpy." My hair was consistently frizzy and unruly, and as a last resort, I'd throw it in a messy bun on top of my head so I didn't have to deal with it. Then, when I would walk into the bathroom after tennis practice or at the end of the day when I got home from school and would see, to my horror, the frizzy little baby hairs I'd missed, I'd sigh in frustration. I always felt unkempt because of my hair; it just wouldn't behave. (If you read my previous book, *The Drybar Guide to Good Hair for All*, you can get a glimpse of the single photograph of me and Mom as she attempted to blow my hair straight with a Conair travel blow-dryer, both of us at the end of our wits.[3])

Back in high school in Boca Raton, Florida, when my days working at Flip's finally ended, I got a job at the Al Stephens hair salon in Town Center Mall (and traded grumpy old customers from Flip's for a grumpy old boss). I was just the receptionist, but I loved working there. This was my first foray into the salon culture, and I was immediately hooked. I loved the energy and how fun and talented the stylists were. It was loud, busy, and chaotic in the best way. I couldn't get enough. I also loved working the front desk, being in charge, and staying busy. Foreshadowing, right?

I watched girls come in with frizzy, wiry, untamable hair like mine and leave with soft, cascading waves. Girls with stringy, waist-length hair left with blunt, healthy-looking bobs. These fabulous transformations exhilarated me, and I felt hopeful that I wouldn't be stuck with my impossible hair forever. The best perk of the job was that sometimes the stylists would even blow out my hair for free. I studied their technique intensely, desperate to understand how to recreate such amazing hair. It looked easy enough.

When I was a kid (all the way into my teens), my mom and I had a Saturday routine that I loved. She would take me with her to the salon for her weekly mani-pedi and hair appointment (cut or color, whatever was needed). Her oh-so-cool hairstylist, Michelangelo—I promise I'm not making that up—would eye my frizzy hair and shake his head, muttering under his breath.

"Can you make it straight?" I'd beg.

He would circle around me like a sculptor surveying a block of clay, trying to figure out how he could make it work. And he did. When I walked out of the salon, I'd have sleek, shiny, straight hair, and I wouldn't wash it for weeks. Man, did I love that hair. It was an absolute treat for me, and I couldn't get enough. Before the days of popular straightening treatments, Michelangelo even tried to do a reverse perm to straighten my unruly locks, but sadly, it didn't work.

I would have rather baked to death in the Florida sun than jump in a pool and risk losing my shampoo commercial–worthy hair. I felt like a different person when my hair was polished and straight. I looked good; therefore I *felt* good. When my hair became frizzy again, I felt messy. It was like walking around with a big coffee stain on your shirt. (For the record, I would later come to love my curly hair as I learned how to style it better. I learned to appreciate and love it much more than I did as a kid.)

Back in those formative years, while I constantly obsessed over hair (not much has changed), it never once occurred to me that I was passionate enough about it to make it into my career. After taking the long way around, with many jobs and moves under my belt, I finally enrolled in beauty school, much to my parents' chagrin. It was a less than stellar spot located in a strip mall (next to The Melting Pot—*yum*) with blinding fluorescent lights, rows of old salon chairs, and a stench of chemicals that would make you light-headed. But God, did I love it. I learned about hair and nails. I found my people, and it turned out my people were eclectic, tattooed hair magicians with mouths like sailors and locks like the Greek pantheon. It was perfect.

I adored the atmosphere and the energy. It was all so much fun. I'd spend most days at school, then head over to assist John Peters, a well-known hair stylist in Florida. I quickly become his right-hand girl. I soaked up all the hair knowledge I could from that local genius and learned how to run a salon, which I didn't realize would serve me so well years later.

I'd never had more fun than working in salons, and somewhere along the way I'd forgotten that.

. . . .

As I mentioned in the previous chapter, when I was talking with Paige several years later, my idea was simple: I wanted to go to women's houses and blow-dry their hair. That was it. No muss, no fuss. No cuts, no color. Just a simple blow-dry to make them feel fabulous.

When I dropped the bomb that I wanted to break our partnership in the event-planning company to start a mobile blowout company, I was worried there would be ramifications. But, like the true friend she was, Paige was completely on board and gave me the confidence I needed to turn this glimmer of an idea into a reality.

"How much would you charge?" she asked.

Bolstered by her vote of confidence, I shrugged. "Forty bucks?"

She grinned. "Two twenties, perfect."

Boom. That was it. My entire business plan. Straight at Home was born. (Back then I thought women mostly wanted their frizzy locks blown straight. Oh, how wrong I was!) This simple idea was my calling card to entrepreneurship, a principle I still carry with me today: When starting a business, don't overthink it. Don't get too far ahead of yourself. Always, *always* start with a great idea.

While I'd taken the long way around to figuring out what I really wanted to do, I knew I had always loved hair. No matter what other diversions I'd taken up, I always went back to hair—even if I was just doing my own. It had been the constant thread through all my past projects and jobs. I would lose track of time and enter a total flow state when working with hair.

Getting back to my roots (literally) was like slipping on a favorite outfit. I felt so good, like I was exactly where I was supposed to be. I created an opportunity for myself to connect with other women and make them feel beautiful—all for an affordable price. (The fact that I just so happened to nab some affluent and brilliant clientele was just icing on the blowout cake.) I was set to combine all my past professional learning experiences—working the floor at Flip's, scheduling and chatting at hair salons, mining the corporate world in New York, and navigating beauty school—all while still getting to be a mom.

> I created an opportunity for myself. Don't wait around for someone else to do it for you.

I started this new venture by first catering to my Yahoo! mom group called PeachHeadz. It was an invite-only mommy resource group that grew into a massive hub of super-interesting women where we could all post about whatever we were doing or needed help or guidance on.

My pitch went something like this: "I'm a stay-at-home mom and a longtime hairstylist. I'll come over and blow out your hair for only $40 while your baby is sleeping!"

Just like that, I started getting *tons* of emails and started building my blowout business mainly by word of mouth. It was definitely a domino effect. Women began introducing me to their friends—lawyers, writers, and actors—and soon I was driving all over LA, meeting women from all walks of life. I loved every second of it. It was exactly what I needed.

If you were one of my first few clients, watching me pull into your driveway in my used Nissan Xterra, you probably didn't get the impression that I was a buttoned-up businesswoman. I'd pull out my ragtag assortment of colorful hair tools and brushes from my duffel bag and loose cans of heat protectant and hair spray from the back seat and hobble awkwardly to the front door. (Oh, how far I've come.)

Gradually, I started nailing the details, like which hair products I loved, which products I needed on deck just in case, and which ones could be left at home. Most of my clients were moms. Some were more stressed and busier than others, but the majority were working moms—and the priority was styling in a way that would last them a few days.

Though I didn't know it at the time, I was creating the foundation for Drybar.

People trusted me, they loved the price, and the feedback was spectacular because I consistently made my clients' hair look *exactly* how they wished it did every day. I knew what they wanted because I knew what *I* always wanted and could never easily and regularly achieve with unruly, textured curls. (What I wouldn't have given to have someone come to my house and blow out my hair for just forty dollars!) When I started getting affluent and celebrity clientele, I thought, *Is this really happening?* I was showing up to the most gorgeous homes in Los Angeles. It definitely made me long for more for myself.

My clients kept spreading the word until I became so busy that I had to start saying no. With all the prep, packing, and driving, there just wasn't enough time in the day for me to drive out to more and more homes in dense LA traffic and pick up my little ones by two or three in the afternoon. I wasn't forcing this growth, by the way; it was all just *happening* and pushing me to make the changes the business needed to thrive. What a gift. I was so grateful for these women.

Finally, instead of me continuing to visit clients at their homes, I knew I had to have them start coming to me. But how?

I began to hint at the idea of a brick-and-mortar location, though I had no property, no real business plan, and no money. Within less than a year, I had support all over metro LA. These women were *behind* me, and I felt empowered to take my business—still called Straight at Home at that point—to the next level. But how?

. . . .

While I was running the business, my mom was moonlighting part-time at Chico's and would babysit children other than mine. One woman she babysat for also had an idea for opening a blow-dry salon concept. I asked my mom to introduce us because I thought it was interesting that she wanted to do something so similar and maybe we could form a partnership, since the idea of doing it alone was very daunting to me.

We chatted—I liked her a lot and thought maybe she would be my partner in what ultimately would become Drybar. However, I quickly learned she did not value what I was bringing to the table. She offered me 5 percent of the company *she* wanted to build.

Um, what?

Seriously, I was floored. *I* was the stylist—the one with years and years of blow-drying and salon experience. Not to mention, I'd been growing my own idea and client base for two years, and she was offering me a teeny cut of what *I'd already built*. It felt pretty shitty.

I called my brother Michael, and after listening quietly to my out-loud processing, he said, "I'll do it with you." I looked at the phone in disbelief, recounting the total shit show of our brief time working together at the Nicole Miller shop in Florida. I didn't want to wreck our relationship again, and I certainly didn't want to end up hating each other.

"You know I don't have any money," I said.

Fully aware he was the only one of us who had been successful thus far, he didn't hesitate. He said, "I'll give you fifty percent sweat equity, and I'll put up all the money."

"*All the money?*" I said excitedly. "As you may know, my dear brother, I'm not good with money."

Even over the phone, I could tell he was smirking. "Lucky for you, *I* am."

"I don't really want to be a CEO," I added. It wasn't that I didn't *want* to run my own company—I just felt like I didn't have enough experience (or, you know, any). Titles meant very little to me. Michael and I would be equal partners regardless of what we were called. We talked about being co-CEOs, but it just didn't appeal to me, and I knew Michael would be so good at it.

"I'll handle it," he said.

"I don't really know how to run a business though."

"We'll figure it out," he said. Michael has always been my biggest fan and number one supporter.

I have to admit, I was freaking out in the best way and couldn't believe we were doing this. I remember Cam saying, "No way Mike is going to actually do this with you." As I write this, my brother is now the world's most doting father to the cutest five-year-old you ever did see—but back then, he was a fast-moving, wheeler-dealer type. Neither of us could wrap our heads around this idea becoming a reality, but we knew that with Michael involved, it was going to happen.

Cam agreed to do all the creative design work and basically invent the brand. He would be the creative leader, Michael would handle the business and financing, and I would focus on the hair quality, running the shops, and handling customer service. It took us about a year of planning. Cam worked tirelessly on the website, usually after the kids were in bed, starting around 10 p.m. and working until 1 a.m. I took care of all the licensing paperwork, ordering towels, finding hair products and tools for the shops, finding kick-ass stylists, and all the mundane shit you have to do when starting a business. This is part of paying your dues, in case you were wondering—if you're looking to start a business, get ready for a lot of boring shit. The trick is to stay focused on your goals.

After my brother fronted $250,000 and Cam and I put in our savings—which was about $50,000, mostly from Cam's 401(k)—I realized we were *all in*. It was an exhilarating and horrifying feeling to watch your bank account go from "nest egg" to "zero" for a big personal investment, but we knew it was right.

I had this feeling in the back of my mind that if it didn't in fact work and we all lost money, we would get back on our feet and figure out something else. After all, we were smart, capable, and hirable people, and I'd never been one to dwell on consequences. Plus, I wasn't afraid of risk. No risk, no reward, right?

. . . .

Fear stands in the way of most things in our lives. Over the years, I have met so many people who are afraid to step out and start their business: "Where do I *start*?" "*How* do I start?" "Is my idea good enough?" "Will people like it?" I could go on and on. I get it; there are a zillion questions we don't have the answers to. But that's half the fun—figuring it out as you go. You would be hard-pressed to find any successful entrepreneur who doesn't agree, as most of us don't know what we are doing at first. But we pay attention; we learn from our missteps and mistakes. We follow our gut. We take a leap, and we learn. And we keep learning.

My advice? Just start.

Worry about all that other shit as you go.

For Drybar, we started with a good idea—an idea that my mobile business had already proven would work on a small scale. I felt confident I could make our first shop work. There was no plan for world domination or anything, but one shop? Totally doable. Good idea? Check. Kinda proven concept? Check. Proving that Drybar would work nationwide? That was another story entirely.

. . . .

From there, we worked backward. I had to adapt to face some unknowns and confront decisions that needed to be made (and that, quite frankly, I didn't have a clue about).

There were so many things we hadn't considered. And even more of a realization that we didn't know what we didn't know. For example, we hired a general contractor, who was a friend of a friend of Cam's. (Shout out to Dean Atkinson; forever grateful to you.) Once we started to dig, we realized connections were everywhere. It was vital to leverage our networks and ask everyone we knew to help connect us.

One thing I've realized is that your personal network is bigger and greater than you probably think it is. And don't be afraid to ask for help. It's humbling, I know, but the worst they can say is no.

We did know that dividing and conquering was the best way to keep the process moving. I was getting a lot of free blowouts (some better than others), in an attempt to find the best stylists for Drybar, while my brother was clocking hours upon hours on the phone with the phone company. (He still waxes poetic about how that process took years off his life.) Together, we scoured LA trying to find the best first outpost for Drybar.

Mind you, this was circa 2009 (right in the end of a major recession), and the stores on the most popular blocks in LA were closing shop. Yet there we were, trying to find a location for a brand-spanking-new blow-dry bar concept. Fat chance. Let's just say, we weren't a shoo-in. Landlords practically laughed in our faces when we presented this unheard-of concept. "You want to just blow-dry hair? In a bar? I don't think that's going to work."

Despite that, we finally found the perfect spot for the first Drybar at Brentwood Gardens in Los Angeles. While it had once been a robust, bustling shopping center, it was now quiet and slow. Michael and I had to guarantee that space personally, which is not the norm for commercial property. But what did we have to lose? (Not much, financially.) That first landlord was a grumpy old man, but he did take a chance on us.

We spent the next six to eight months preparing to bring this brand-new concept to life. I *loved* this process: the building phase. It's exhilarating to work toward creating something—to go from concept to an actual business.

Cam, Michael, and I split the responsibilities. Michael spent hours dealing with all the legal mumbo jumbo, negotiating lease terms, and doing a bunch of other shit I still don't know or care about.

I was busy finding towel vendors, talking to the cosmetology board (which is a government agency that wasn't very into me), finding the best products and tools, and seeking great and kind stylists (entitled stylists need not apply). All the while, Cam was developing the website and all the creative collateral for the shop—things like our original gift certificates for one free blowout that were a play on drink coasters (everything was bar themed) that had "Lucky B*tch" or "Someone Loves You" written on them.

People went bananas for those. We literally couldn't keep the "Lucky B*tch" coasters in stock. For years, I didn't leave the house without a bundle of these in my purse. I would give them away at every opportunity I got: to the girls at the checkout, whenever I was shopping, to my friends, to other moms. If you ran into Alli Webb, chances are you were getting a free blowout.

That behavior may have been influenced by watching *The Oprah Winfrey Show* as a girl every single day after school with Oreos and a glass of milk. I adored Oprah's generosity, and I, too, loved surprising people and making their day with something free and unexpected.

I have to give Michael credit for this too. When we were under construction on the first Brentwood shop, Michael wanted to put a sign on the front window that said, "First 250 people to sign up on the website will get a *free* blowout!"

"*What?* Are you crazy?" I said to him. "We won't make any money."

In hindsight, it was such small thinking on my part. As it turned out, it was a brilliant business tactic and would serve as an incredible tool to jump-start our email list—which is gold, y'all.

When you're in the early phases of building a business, you're always in a state of kind of figuring it out—learning by failing, asking questions, calling people, asking favors, leveraging your network, and utilizing people around you. I'm a pretty open person, and talking about my Drybar journey was my favorite subject back then. It was sort of like when you have a new baby—I loved sharing it all, and I wanted to inspire other budding entrepreneurs on their journeys too.

However, that would backfire on me a bit. Within months, there were several attempts to knock off our blow-dry bar concept. But I'd been doing hair and blowouts for the better part of my life, and I knew I had something they didn't. I knew the industry backward and forward. It was my passion. It was my *thing*. No matter who tried to knock me off, I knew they wouldn't be able to take that away. I felt uniquely qualified to be at the helm of what was becoming a blowout empire. Who knew? *I* did.

Also, for the first time in my life, it seemed that people around me—friends and family included—wanted to be part of something *I* had built. After searching so long for my thing, it was an incredible feeling.

I reveled in it. My entire life, I'd tried all these different jobs, inevitably walking away from each one when it didn't feel just right anymore. I felt like the Goldilocks of business, trying things on but never feeling completely at home despite working hard.

Then, one day, it dawned on me as I was standing in Drybar Brentwood, soaking it all in, that the reason I had always walked away was because those other jobs had been in service of dreams that weren't *mine*.

This was my dream.

And I was going to make it spectacular.

Lessons I've Learned

Be Open and Welcoming to Feedback from Everyone: There Is Always More to Learn

Hearing negative feedback sucks.

From your partner. From your friends. From your coworkers. In no universe does it *not* sting to be told that something you have worked your ass off for has fallen short. It's the worst. And this is where our glorious ego comes in and wants to fight for us. *Thanks, ego, but please step aside and allow me to grow and learn from this and not take it personally.* (I know, easier said than done.)

Being open to feedback, personal or professional, is a practice—a learned intention to stop, take in the information, maybe go on a walk, take some deep breaths, and come back, open to hearing what someone else is feeling.

You don't always have to agree, but I implore you to at least consider what someone else is observing about a shortcoming in your life or business.

I also firmly believe most people in life tell you what you want to hear, so that one brave soul who sticks out their neck to *help you* by being honest is probably representing a bunch of other people. If I had been honest with Cam about how I was feeling before I married him, my life would have been different. If I had one friend who had looked me in the eye and said, "You're not ready to get married, and here's why," would I have chosen a different path?

Being open in your personal life can bleed over to your work. If you are the type of person who openly and warmly welcomes feedback from everyone, then you'll get a lot more out of people and ultimately will create a pretty rad work environment where employees aren't afraid to share.

None of Us Has All the Answers, So Just Keep Going

You are not alone here.

Everyone has felt self-doubt and that "Oh shit, I don't know what the fuck I'm doing" moment, week, or month. Just like life, business ebbs and flows. It's certainly not a linear path. The will and persistence to keep going, to keep searching for new ways to make something work, is the key and what sets successful entrepreneurs apart from those who can't take the heat.

It is unbelievably stressful to be holding the bag when business is slow, and you just can't seem to crack the code on why it's not working and yet you believe in this thing so fiercely—but you have people to pay. Keep going.

Keep trying things.

Just keep going.

Empires Aren't Built on the Shoulders of One Person: You Need a Team

You are only as good as your team.

This lesson is hard for entrepreneurs—at least it was for me. While I always valued the people around me, in the early days of

Drybar, I had the overwhelming (and wrong) idea that I had to have all the answers. I thought I had to be a fearless leader, yet I was essentially figuring it out as I went; most of us are doing just that.

I also had a pretty tight grip on the business and was sure no one could do it as well as I could. Wrong again. Sure, Drybar was my baby, and I was the visionary, but it took me a long time to ask for real help from anyone other than Michael and Cam.

It was my brother who recognized early on that we needed help, and he often said, "This amazing business is ours to fuck up." He was right. We needed help in all the ways.

In full transparency, it took us a long time to get the right team in place. Don't be afraid to allow yourself the time and space to find the right team; it doesn't happen overnight.

We're all "*imposters*" when we start; that's how experts are created.

What does success look like to you?

....

....

....

....

....

....

....

....

....

....

....

....

....

....

....

....

....

....

....

....

Chapter Four

The Truth About Overnight Success

If you don't have a large investment to help
build your business, start small, grow slowly, and
keep an eye out for big opportunities.

A week before we opened our first location, *Daily Candy*[4] featured the news of Drybar with a pithy headline that read "Hot Air Is Blowing into LA," and appointments started pouring in.

A few weeks before opening, Michael and I were having lunch at the Coral Tree Café in Brentwood (best Chinese chicken salad west of the 405!), which was just down the street from the shop, when suddenly our BlackBerries (yup, this was pre-iPhones, kids) simultaneously started sending a flurry of appointment alerts.

We assumed it was some sort of glitch; something had to have gone awry. I thought for sure I was going to have to call SpaBooker, our appointment booking platform, to see what was going on.

It turns out there was no glitch. The *Daily Candy* article ran, and people were flocking to book a blowout. Like, *a shitload* of people. At the time, online booking was such a new concept that scheduling was a frenzy, and we were completely overwhelmed. Thanks again, *Daily Candy*. You are a big part of my story.

"Michael, the books are almost full," I squealed. Then reality set in as I realized I didn't have enough stylists to fill all eight chairs all day, every day. *Panic.* Spoiler alert: this problem would turn out to be one of our biggest hurdles for years to come. Good ol' supply and demand, folks. Demand was almost never a problem, but finding great stylists proved to be one of the biggest, if not the biggest, challenges we would face.

. . . .

We opened that first day promptly at 9 a.m., and the ladies started rolling in for their appointments. What. A. Thrill. We were so busy, in fact, that we didn't even *know how to do what we were doing.* We expected to have a little time to figure out the ins and outs of the business, but the shop went from 0 to 100 instantly, and we were overbooked and understaffed (which was actually pretty amazing, but still left us all thinking, *Oh shit.*).

I had to take charge of the floor, too, because, believe it or not, back then, I didn't think I needed a manager; I figured I could just handle it all. Wrong! I hunkered down at the first chair (closest to the front desk—check-in and checkout) so I could simultaneously do blowouts, keep a close eye on the front desk, greet clients, and train my other eye on the row of stylists and clients. It was bananas, but I loved every single second of that chaos. I can't emphasize enough the pure joy and sense of accomplishment this whole experience brought me. I *loved* that we were busy and that stylists *wanted* to work at Drybar and that clients *wanted* to come in.

I was making conversation with excited women headed off to big meetings, busy mamas getting a needed break, or giddy girls prepping for first dates. No matter who the client was, I realized we were delivering a very valuable and important service: confidence. Women walked in feeling one way (all business or very serious), and they left with a renewed pep in their step, feeling like they could conquer the world. That may sound dramatic, but it's true. The transformation we saw over and over again in these women was remarkable. We were changing lives one blowout at a time. This idea turned out to be way more important than any of us realized.

I couldn't imagine doing more worthwhile work than that.

. . . .

Meanwhile, the phone kept ringing off the hook. A storm of people hurried in and out. It was a madhouse, and I quickly realized I needed help. A lot of help.

At the time, Michael wasn't full-time at Drybar, and neither was Cam. It was just me and my amazing sister-in-law, Sarah Landau, figuring it all out day by day. Sarah is Michael's wife—well, ex-wife now, although that's a really long and beautiful story for another day.

Sarah was there with me around the clock in those early days doing whatever needed to be done and would eventually take on the role of spirit director. Isn't that the coolest title? On the regular, she would make the rounds to as many shops as possible and connect with all the stylists and bartenders (that's what we called the receptionists at the front desk) to understand what was going on behind the scenes and get to know the needs of everyone. It was an incredibly valuable and important role that really served the company.

In the middle of that first day, I remember calling Michael and Cam, in tears of joy and disbelief. "Oh my God, we did it. This fucking thing worked!" We were beside ourselves with our success, and I was overwhelmed by what we had accomplished. It felt like a dream.

People were loving Drybar and were counting on us for the big and small events in their lives. We kinda felt like the hot club you couldn't get into, which felt cool for a minute but was not ideal for a budding business. In those first few weeks and months, it felt like we were pissing off clients who couldn't get an appointment rather than making them happy. I would even go so far as to pull out barstools from the break room to accommodate disgruntled clients (which went against my branding code of ethics). I wanted to get everyone in so badly, it pained me to turn people away. I felt honored to give the gift of great hair because I knew all too well how amazing the end result felt. But we simply couldn't handle all the demand. (I know, I know. What a great problem to have.) The point I'm making is this: every turn in business is a struggle. Even when you have success, it's just followed by new struggles. Hopefully you're wiser, more resourceful, and more connected to meet these wonderful new demands, but the struggle of expansion *never* really goes away.

This was about the time I begged Michael to make this his full-time gig and find us more shops, because one location was just not going to cut it. He was in, and off we went to build this crazy empire none of us had seen coming.

. . . .

At this point, Michael and I were talking around the clock. Our little business was booming. We were positively giddy and a little stressed and a lot tired (but mostly giddy).

One day, I called Michael, and when he answered, it was perfectly silent in the background. It was alarming and glorious how foreign silence sounded to me. I had gotten used to the white noise hum of blow-dryers and blasting music.

Ironically, we had both called a local spa to book massages (this was pre-Squeeze, my newest venture; more to come on that) because we were exhausted and needed a breather. We both marveled at how quiet it was when we booked our massages. The booking process was seamless and relaxing. We wanted *that* experience for our clients. But how? With eight blow-dryers raging, music blasting, movies playing, and women chatting, we knew we simply couldn't create that over-the-top experience for our clients calling the store to book.

With the chaos of the phone ringing constantly, we knew we had to pull the landline from the shop because we couldn't deliver a great interaction with the clients in the shop *and* talk with clients on the phone at the same time.

The solution? A remote call center! *Oof!* I wasn't very excited to be in the virtual call center business. It would take a lot of training to make this work, but it was far better than the alternative, which was letting the phone inside the shop ring and ring and then go to voicemail and *then* having to call people back. Ugh, can you imagine what a disaster that was? I just wanted to be in the shop, not trying to figure out a whole other business. (But I knew *someone* had to do it.)

It was a challenge to get great people on the phone and figure out ways for the shop and the phone agents to sync up—and, understandably, clients didn't love not being able to call the shop directly. I understood this frustration, but it couldn't be helped.

This was a tough challenge that would also go on for years, but once we made the decision to take the phones out of the shop, we focused on greeting our customers the right way. I am a *huge* proponent of being greeted properly when I walk into a business. Sadly, I feel this is something most businesses do not do well. A proper greeting is crucial. Essential. It's everything!

Over-the-top customer service was a value I learned early on from watching my brilliant parents run their clothing store. Flips. and it is still something I carry with me today.

If you ever worked with me at Drybar, you may remember how much I talked about the greeting. If you wanted to irritate the shit out of me, you could greet someone with a very flat and cold, "Do you have an appointment?" Um, nails on a chalkboard. The worst.

Instead, I coached bartenders to greet clients with a different approach, such as, "Hey, Sally, nice to see you! Let me get you checked in. Would you like a mimosa or glass of water?" Or, if they didn't know the client's name, they could say, "Hi there, welcome. It's so nice to see you! How can I help you today?"

While I was dealing with real-time shop issues, Michael was on the hunt for another location. The two of us were definitely finding our grooves and respective lanes. I slowly started to learn how to delegate and what kind of boss I wanted to be—and more importantly, what kind of boss I *needed* to be.

I wanted to be open and approachable. I wanted to be in the trenches with my team and show them no job was too small for me or anyone. I wanted people to know they could simultaneously have fun and relax a little while working hard. I wanted to create an environment where stylists felt they were a part of something special and could be themselves while respecting me and the work too.

I also realized what type of people I wanted working alongside me at Drybar. Instinctively, I knew it would be important to cultivate a fun, friendly, open environment—a place where people felt they belonged. I strongly felt that if the stylists were happy, the clients would be happy; and if the clients were happy, the whole thing would work a lot better. We would all collectively benefit from that trickle-down effect. Most of us spend more time at our jobs than we do with our families, so let's make it the absolute best it can be, right? While I was technically the boss, it was also important to generate camaraderie. I made sure my people could see me not only making the big decisions but also still sweeping the floor. (Yes, I even cleaned the bathrooms. Many times.)

Originally, I hired only a few stylists (maybe fifteen) to work the floor, which I learned was not anywhere near enough. It was never enough. I desperately needed quality stylists, yet I was the pickiest client you could imagine, so it was very challenging to find people who were not only great stylists but extremely oriented to customer service as well.

When we opened our second and third Drybar shops in Studio City and West Hollywood, they were dead. Yes, that's right: zero clients. WTF? Brentwood was busy all the time, so why weren't women flocking to our other locations?

Well, because nothing is easy, y'all. Even though we initially had a ton of success, we had to go back to the drawing board for the next two shops. We got scrappy. We ran a Groupon. I went to all the local school fairs selling discounted blowouts to get women in the door. We asked friends to come in for a free blow-dry and post about it. You name it; we tried it. And it worked. No matter your roadblocks: Just. Keep. Going. You will get there.

Another big difference at Drybar was for clients to be able to get a great blowout from *all* of our stylists, not just see the same stylist week after week. For this concept to work, we needed clients to shift around between a few or several different stylists, not just go to their favorite one. While this was a big gamble, ultimately it paid off.

A woman would walk in, and for just thirty-five dollars, her whole persona would change. It wasn't just her hair that changed but her entire demeanor. She was all of a sudden the best version of herself. She felt different, better.

I started adopting my own personal business mantra: "It's not just blowouts we're selling; it's the happiness and confidence that comes from a great blowout."

During the opening, and the weeks following, a smattering of celebrity clientele (Zooey Deschanel, Jennifer Garner, Gwyneth Paltrow, Julia Roberts, Emma Roberts, and Maria Shriver, just to name a few) really upped our "it" factor. These were women who graced the big and small screens, who lived lives I couldn't imagine, and they were coming to *my* place of business. They loved Drybar.

I assumed they all had big fancy stylists and could afford to have those stylists come to their homes for upward of three hundred dollars per blowout, no sweat. But after talking to them and asking point-blank, "Why do you come to Drybar when you have so many other options?" the answer was always the same: "I love it here. The atmosphere is fun and lively, your stylists are great, I love watching the movies, and the price is right. Why wouldn't I?" Everyone loves a good deal and a great atmosphere, no matter how much money they have.

This was music to my ears, and I would never tire of hearing this feedback.

It was all such a whirlwind, and I totally got swept up. Suddenly, I was traveling on the regular to open new shops around the county—so much so that when my son Grant was around about 7, he would say, "Mommy, why don't you open up more stores in LA, so you don't have to leave so much?"

Cue the tears.

I considered that. Certainly, I wanted to be home more with my boys, but I was convinced that doing what I loved and felt called to do (for arguably the first time in my life) was making me a better mom. I would explain this to my kids over and over until they were old enough to really understand it: "This is important for me to do because I really enjoy it, and I will be a happier, better mom to you and Kit if I'm doing what I need to do for me." I was building something for myself and something for them, and I felt purposeful in a way I hadn't since giving birth. (Sidenote: I now get to hang out with my boys a lot more than I did back then, and you better believe I relish every second of it. I also enjoy the teenage years *way* more than the toddler ones. If you know, you know.)

Before Drybar, Cam had been the breadwinner in our household, but suddenly—within months—I was in the public spotlight, and I was getting all the notoriety for Drybar. This was an adjustment all the way around. My travel schedule got crazy, and even though my mom carried a lot of the weight during those first few years by helping with the boys, it was taxing on Cam too. He was home alone a lot with two little kids. The resentment started to build. He was sad and frustrated that I often left him alone with the kids. I think it was a combo of caring for two young children by himself and not getting to go with me.

For me to be doing all the travel solo in the business we built together felt shitty to him, but instead of really talking it through and working through it, we just built up more anger and resentment. I knew it was there, but I didn't want to face it.

Now I understand how important it is for couples to debrief nightly as a way to clear any resentments or upset. Talk about them, get them out there, and learn how to be better and do better by each other. That kind of relational work never occurred to me or Cam then, so the resentment continued to build, and it would eventually come out very sideways.

It was a hard spot for Cam. And while I know he was genuinely happy to see me thrive, I'm sure it was tough to feel a bit left behind. I understood it, I really did, but I was torn, too, because I loved traveling and all the attention and positivity that came from this business. It felt like a dream come true that I didn't even know I'd had.

Somewhere around this point, I started to realize that maybe I couldn't have success in business *and* motherhood *and* maintain a happy marriage. I missed my boys constantly, but I was also on this gigantic high that clouded everything else. There was so much forward momentum that I really didn't have time to process this realization or do much about it in the moment.

I was afraid to slow down, afraid of not continuing to grow and build, afraid of what I was feeling as my marriage began to fade and crumble. I was terrified of destroying the facade. I liked the way my life looked from the outside: Cool, super-talented husband! Two cute boys with cute hair! A thriving business! It all looked great on paper, and I felt too ashamed to upset the balance by revealing that my marriage *wasn't* great. I felt like a massive failure behind my massive success.

I didn't want that facade to reveal what I was really feeling. It seemed like too much was at risk, that I had too much to lose. Every time I imagined airing my truth like a bag of dirty laundry, I froze. *What will people think?*

So I told myself to "just keep swimming, swimming, swimming." (Thanks, Dory.[5]) I now know that smashing down all my feelings contributed to what would become my great depression circa 2018. (Stay tuned for that delightful chapter.)

Seemingly overnight, Drybar really blew up (pun intended). We were incredibly busy: busy building the business, busy raising money, busy hiring tons of people, busy working like dogs. It was complete and amazing insanity.

And again, despite the stress, I fucking loved it.

For me, juggling all these components of my life, I knew that something was going to have to give.

And I knew just what that something was. Even though I was terrified of it, even though I wanted to ignore the issues in my marriage and hope they went away, I had to face our problems.

I didn't like who I was becoming. I was bitchy, and Cam and I would fight all the time in front of the boys, but I took it too far and I regret that. What I realize now is how important it is to model a healthy, loving, and generous relationship vs. the "let's stay together no matter how miserable we are" model. Even though I no longer felt like the best version of myself within my marriage, I was still terrified to discover who I would be outside of it.

But just like in business, this was a necessary risk I was (eventually) willing to take.

Lessons I've Learned

It Can Be Intoxicating to Grow Fast, but It's Also Easy to Lose Sight of What Made You Grow in the First Place

There is no *one* right way to grow a business; each one is unique.

But I can tell you that in my experience, growing Drybar was like being on a rocket ship from day one. We had so much demand and so many copycats on our tail that we felt a lot of pressure to grow big, grow fast, and operate at light speed.

The competition gaining on us was certainly an important factor for our growth. We wanted to stay the leader in this space. As a result, we made a lot of mistakes. We were growing at such an accelerated and dangerous pace that it felt like the wheels were starting to come off.

It's important when you are growing fast to keep a pulse check on what made your business unique in the first place. Don't lose that authenticity in favor of a short-term goal of making more money or growing too fast because you feel pressure (whether internally or from investors).

Goals are fun to chase; priorities aim you toward the frenzy; principles keep you sane. Always start with your guiding principles. No matter the pace or challenge, what will you always use to filter your decisions? How will you keep loyalty in an expanding team? Prove to them that some basic principles will never change.

Even big businesses can grow slowly and intentionally; it's simply about figuring out what you want out of your business in the long run.

You Can't Be Everything to Everyone: Make Sure to Fill Company Seats With People Who Know What They're Doing and Are Happy to Be There

Because we were growing so fast, we had new shops opening all the time.

While these openings were incredibly fun, we made the mistake of having almost everyone in the company come to each opening; this came from a good, inclusive place, but ultimately, it was like five-year-olds playing soccer. Everyone wanted the ball, and it just wasn't working.

This was right around the time we brought in a professional CEO—someone who had *actual* experience growing a company in a thoughtful manner. John Hefner, aka Papa John (not to be confused with the pizza chain), felt like the only adult in the room, and we knew we needed real help putting systems in place and getting more organized around growth and scale.

When we started Drybar, I wanted Michael to be the CEO, as I wasn't interested in that role. I think this is where a lot of founders struggle, because they feel like they should *want* to be CEO.

I didn't (and still don't) regret that decision. Not everyone is cut out to be CEO. If you are, then great, go get 'em. But if not, be open to allowing others who may be more qualified and have more experience to help you. This is one of my most valued lessons: recognizing my highest and best use.

Let me share an observation here: businesses don't usually fail because their idea wasn't good enough. More often, a business doesn't work because a founder didn't get that while they are a brilliant visionary, they are a poor executive. You can't recruit brilliant people if you're the proverbial emperor with no clothes.

Hiring John as CEO changed the game for us. He wasn't emotionally attached to Drybar the way Michael, Cam, and I were. Michael and I fell in love with John in the very first interview. Not every CEO is comfortable in a founder-run organization (don't forget that!). John had worked in several and was ready to walk in lockstep with us, unlike a lot of CEOs who want to come in like a bulldozer and take over.

It was a beautiful partnership with John that made all the difference in growing Drybar.

When You Want to Grow, Sometimes You Need to Slow Down to Speed Up

When we had about eleven shops open, I realized that my *go, go, go* personality was becoming a liability, not an asset.

Not everyone operated from that same sense of urgency, and because I didn't slow down, I expected everyone else to keep up. Because of this, the cracks started to show in other facets of my life.

I felt like slowing down would somehow compromise my belief or passion in Drybar. I didn't take time to sit back and look at everything objectively. I didn't take time to rest. I didn't take time to rethink my priorities.

I wanted to build an empire, and I thought I had to practically kill myself to make that happen.

I learned so many lessons on my journey of surrounding myself with people who were less impetuous than me. Less impulsive. Less hustle-oriented. Less focused on grinding it out. Less impatient. People who complemented my strengths but had their own way of doing things.

That founder mentality of "perfection at all costs" (plus a "working yourself into the ground" mentality) can be detrimental. It's vital to invite in some counterbalance.

Because of this, it's imperative to know what your strengths and weaknesses are, and then hire people who fill in the gaps where you could use some help.

You are only as strong as the team you build, and sometimes taking a bit longer to build the right team (or restructure it) is one of the most important assets to building a bigger brand.

Pay attention to what's working and what's not working.

What does success look like if no one is watching?

Part Two

Your Mess Is Your Magic

Chapter Five

When Business Booms, Someone's Getting Divorced

When shit hits the fan, just let it all fall apart. We aren't made to keep running like robots until we burn out. Take time to rest, reflect, and recharge.

As my business blew up, so did my personal life.

Like, *really* blew up.

As I grappled with my growing discontent in my marriage, I continued to get booked on TV shows, business was soaring, and to the outside world, it appeared like I had my shit together.

But news flash: I really didn't.

Instead of admitting that to myself, I told my publicists and agents that I wanted to do more TV shows and start building my own profile, leveraging what I had built in Drybar because I knew I would someday move on from this role into a new one. I knew we were going to eventually sell the company—and then what? (We'll get to that later!) I realized part of that feeling was because I didn't want to feel "stuck" in my real life. Reality can be a bitch, though I now realize I was searching for a whole new purpose so I could ignore what it was I was actually feeling.

Because Drybar had soared to new heights and we had raised so much money and had hired so many amazing people, I wasn't needed in the day-to-day hustle and bustle like I used to be. I wasn't as busy as I had been for the last seven or eight years. In short, I was panicking.

If I wasn't busy every second of the day, then what was my

purpose? Something big and dark was gnawing at my conscience, until slowly but surely I began to wake up. I realized that I could no longer let distractions rule my whole world. A feeling I had been ignoring for many years was finally catching up, and there was no more hiding; the charade was up.

· ·

It was clear I wasn't getting what I wanted or needed from my marriage. Neither of us were. Somehow, Cam and I had crossed the lines of what a wife and husband were supposed to be, muddling our identities. Cam was what I'd call "metrosexual"— painting his nails, wearing overalls, living a creative life—and I admired his style. But as the big boss, I was in charge of things all day, every day; so at home, I wanted someone else to take the reins. I longed for a chivalrous guy who took care of me.

Instead of talking honestly about what we each needed, our conversations continued to go something like this: I would say, "I want you to take care of me, Cam," to which Cam would reply, "Well, Alli, I want you to take care of me." Fair enough. I don't really remember the conversation going much beyond this. For the record, I do believe couples should take care of each other, but I personally wanted to live much more in my feminine than masculine back then. (I just didn't realize that yet.)

We refused to compromise until, finally, I hit a breaking point. At the start of a business trip to Nashville, then on to Atlantic City to judge the Miss America Pageant, I was sitting in Los Angeles International Airport, barefaced, clad in compression pants and an oversized sweatshirt, ready to nap, when *bam*, a hot guy appeared from thin air. He looked like he just walked out of any girl's fantasy rock band, and he *made fucking eyes at me*.

Surely he's not looking at me, I thought. *Wait! Shit! He is!*

My gut clenched. Something dormant sprung to life. (Hint: it was my vagina.) I tried to suppress my inner seventeen-year-old girl and proceeded to board my plane for my business trip like a proper boss.

It had been *years* since I had felt much of an attraction to another human being, and I had simply resigned myself to the idea that maybe I was asexual. I brushed away the feeling over and over again. I simply took this fleeting moment of desire as a reminder that I was still capable of being attracted to someone, and that felt surprisingly good.

After I took my seat in first class and got set up to sleep the entire flight, Hot Drummer Guy sat *right next to me*—as if I were actually in my own rom com. I mean, are you kidding me, universe?

Though technically I wasn't doing anything wrong, the swell of attraction took me by surprise, because this guy was so different from Cam. He had lots of tattoos (back then, Cam had none), effortlessly unkempt hair, and that rugged rock-star look. We ended up talking the entire flight and exchanged information—or, you know, Instagram handles.

Once we got off the plane, I said goodbye. A thousand imagined scenarios flickered through my brain. *Stop, Alli—just stop. You are a married woman.*

As I watched him walk away, something big swirled inside my chest. I thought, *Am I contemplating an affair?* It all felt so out-of-body, so insane, and definitely not real. *No,* I tried to reassure myself, *you are not this person. You are Cam's wife.* This was on repeat in my head.

Suddenly, Hot Drummer Guy stopped, turned back, and began walking toward me, and got so close I could feel the heat from his body. I envisioned him marching right up to me and saying something like, "Have dinner with me tonight; otherwise I won't be able to get you out of my head."

I held my breath as he stopped right in front of me, my heart thumping madly in my chest. He grinned and raked a hand through his hair.

"I forgot my luggage," he said. (Note to self: life is not a rom com.)

While I was bummed he did not profess his desire to see me that night, the fact that he forgot his luggage meant he was clearly distracted and kinda into me, no?

Regardless, he was going to need to take his bags with him. I was surprised by how badly I wanted him to take something else with him—*me*.

From Nashville, I flew on to Atlantic City, where I met someone else I completely clicked with—a very well-known personality (who shall remain nameless). Man, did we hit it off. We were instantly friends, or so I told myself. We flirted, took photos, hugged, and joked around—and pictures were posted on social media. Stupid idea.

When I boarded a flight bound for home, I was more confused than ever. After one business trip, I was currently embroiled in not one, but *two* emotional affairs, which felt as bad to me as having a physical affair. (Personally, I think it *is* as bad.)

Why did meeting new people—correction: *new men*—feel so good if I was married? Sure, I wasn't in a particularly passionate marriage, but I'd taken vows, and, up until that point, I'd kept them.

When I arrived home, Cam knew something was up. When you've been with someone for seventeen years, you *always* know when something is going on.

We went on our nightly walk after dinner, and it turned out, while I was away, people had been sending him pictures of me from Instagram with the, *ahem*, famous guy, and, even with our marriage in a total freefall, he couldn't help himself from trying to pull our parachute.

"So, what's going on?" he asked.

I took a breath and swallowed. "Well, it was a weird trip."

"If by *weird*, you mean taking pictures with that Hot Famous Guy,[6] then yes, I agree."

Even as he called it out, honestly, I couldn't wipe the shit-eating grin off my face. What was actually *wrong* with me? Did I not have a heart? I tried to play it cool, but I was just backing myself into a corner. I tried to remind myself that years ago, Cam had actually had a millisecond of sex on a business trip with someone else, which he immediately told me about. (A story for another day.) Shouldn't I have been allowed some harmless flirting?

No.

I knew then that our marriage was in real trouble. But I played it off, saying that I liked being on the road, that I wanted to lean in more to that part of my life, and that I wanted to be seen in ways I hadn't before. Cam wasn't fully buying it, though, and I could tell something in me had shifted. As we circled back toward our house, he stopped before we went in and really stared at me.

"Maybe this isn't forever," he finally admitted.

The admission made me gasp—but in relief, not horror. Instead of feeling sad, it was as though the sky was opening, and I was suddenly, simply, allowed to maybe leave. Start over. Begin again. His admission felt like a release. (Although it wasn't—more on that soon.)

We'd had sixteen years of a mostly beautiful marriage, with wild ups and downs (and constant jokes about divorce), and I think we had assumed we would stay together no matter what. If I'm being honest with myself, I'd long been convinced that he would leave me after the kids moved out and wondered if I secretly felt the need to beat him to the punch. The truth was, I was really scared of being too old to find someone else. I realize now that this is silly, but at the time, after watching my parents never find love again after they divorced in their fifties, I was terrified of walking that same, lonely path.

But when Cam admitted our marriage maybe wasn't forever, I realized that everything *could* change—that there was a difference between *talking* about divorce and actually going through with it.

· ·

The next day, I went to my best friend Paige's house and talked to her all damn day about it, all while simultaneously texting with Hot Drummer Guy and Hot Famous Guy from my whirlwind national tour.

I asked Paige, "What should I do?"

She said, "Well, you've been unhappy for a long time. What do you *want* to do?"

"Have I been unhappy?" I asked, but I knew she was right. There was that gnawing feeling again that would not let up, even though I'd pushed it away time and time again. "But I can't imagine leaving Cam," I said. "And the boys! How can I do that to them?"

Both of the men I'd met on my recent trip were asking me if I was considering leaving my husband, and I was responding in equal parts fear and giddiness. It was a very odd and exhilarating experience. I was filled with guilt and did not want to be That Person. I had to face my fears and take action. It all felt crazy, like my life was about to blow up.

After hours of back-and-forth with Paige, I knew what I needed to do. Truth be told, I had known that morning when I kissed Cam goodbye. I had been hurrying to the garage to leave for the day. Cam came out to say bye, and I kissed him as fast as I could, got in the car, and left. When we parted, I somehow knew it would be the last time I would ever kiss my husband. This was a cataclysmic moment, a turning point that would lead to an amazing transformation and an even more awesome responsibility.

Mentally, I already felt released from my marriage as a result of the conversation we had the night before. Cam had said those magic words—"maybe this isn't forever"—and to me, that felt like a sign for me to go, to sever the marriage, to finally throw in the towel. I know he hadn't necessarily meant or wanted that, but it was the underbelly of that conversation that changed the fabric of my life.

I had been in limbo for so long. With a single conversation, I had this tremendous sense of clarity that I was *done*; a switch had flipped, and I knew deep down I could no longer stay in this relationship where I was not fulfilled or happy.

Finally, I texted my therapist: "We need to come see you. And it has to be tonight."

She agreed to a last-minute, late-night emergency session, as did Cam. When we were seated in her office, my heart pounding out of my chest, Cam and I looked at each other. I could tell that he thought we were there to start some work on repairing our relationship (again).

"Why don't you start?" he said.

Gulp. I looked at our therapist and back at Cam and said, confidently, "I think I need to explore other things."

Cam's mouth dropped open as he sat beside me, shifting to turn and *really* look at me. After (some of) the shock wore off, he nodded and said, "I'm really proud of you. I know how hard this is for you."

What? Cue the gospel music and the birds chirping. This was going to be a breeze. I was home free!

After we dissected some issues and laid it all out on the table, Cam said, "I'd love for us to be like your parents. We can be close friends like Roz and Phil."

My parents had gotten divorced when I was in my thirties, and in a weird plot twist, I then learned that they'd had an open marriage, which was the shock of all shocks. The moment they told me that bombshell, my idyllic childhood came rushing back to mind. *Was it all a lie? Were my parents doing weird, kinky things with strangers behind closed doors?*

Now, here I was, in shock again. I was elated that Cam wanted us to be friends. We could tell each other all about the people we are dating, hang out, and keep raising our boys together! A win-win for everyone! I loved the idea (and still do) because Cam is one of the best men I have ever known, and I desperately wanted us to stay connected.

But I'd gotten ahead of myself. (Shocker.)

That night, I left the therapist's office hopeful, thinking that divorce just might be the answer to every marriage's problem. Unfortunately, the understanding and acceptance Cam had shown in our session didn't last.

I know, I know. You probably saw that coming.

. . . .

In the subsequent days and weeks, Cam got sad. He cried. Then he got angry. Like, *really* angry. That glorious dream therapy session had evaporated, and shit started spiraling. Even the night right after our session, we got confused about the sleeping arrangement. The next morning, while I was packing for another trip and wearing just a bra and underwear, Cam walked in on me. "Oh shit," he said, averting his eyes. "Should I leave?"

These were the moments that hurt the most because the severing was starting to feel real and so foreign to us both. There were so many questions. Should we still sleep in the same bed? Should we see each other naked? Should we opt for a formal separation? When would we tell the kids? *What* would we tell the kids?

We decided to wait until some of the initial anger and confusion subsided before we told the boys. We made up some shit about having to travel for work (which the boys later told me they knew was bullshit, because *kids always know*!). I did, however, have to go to QVC for a show a day after we decided to separate, and I'll never forget pacing that long-ass hallway in Pennsylvania on the phone with Cam and our therapist trying to figure out when and how to tell the boys. Talk about rough.

Our therapist gave us the best advice that I'm beyond grateful for and which I think every divorced person should consider to be the holy grail. She said, "Whatever you do, keep it amicable and do not assign blame to each other. If the boys feel like one of you left the other, or one parent is suffering and devastated, then their natural instinct will be to protect the other parent. This will only damage them."

. . . .

Things got even more awkward real fast, and I found myself slipping into an all-consuming depression. Everything I'd known, everything I'd built my whole life, was crumbling. *Who am I? Where do I go? What do I do now?* I had more than just myself to worry about; I had two kids. Two dependent humans needed both of us, and I was afraid of messing up their lives for good.

There was guilt at every turn. It was largely self-inflicted. *Am I ruining my family? Our lives?* But there was also guilt from Cam about how my desire to end the marriage was selfish. And let's not forget the guilt from my family. My mother begged me, "Don't leave Cam."

The craziest part was that I was a mess, and I couldn't put my finger on why. I was excited by the prospect of finally being free to, you know, *explore* other things, but being on my own felt more challenging than I could have imagined.

Even though I believed we did the right thing separating, Cam was angry with me, and there was no way he was going to co-parent (despite that "oh, let's be like your parents" comment in the therapist's office). I understood his anger, and for the first time in my life, I didn't retaliate. I knew he was in pain because *I* was in pain. There was no easy fix. It was hard, and it sucked for both of us. We both were suffering a tremendous loss—a death, really, although it would take me about a year to fully comprehend that a breakup is a lot like a death.

It wasn't until I had the good fortune of meeting Lee Harris, author of the book *Energy Speaks*, that it finally sunk in (isn't it amazing how we won't accept certain things until we are actually ready to see them?). Back then, I would tell anyone I came into contact with how sad and devastated I was (also it was written all over my face, as I had lost thirty pounds!), but I didn't really understand why. When I met Lee, we had a very brief conversation in which he delicately explained to me that there was essentially a big black hole in my life, an empty space where my husband used to be. The energy of having a partner was now gone, and it would take some time and grieving to refill that space. Mind blown.

In my experience, the sooner I can name something that is happening to me, the lighter it becomes. It's really freeing and far healthier than avoidance, my drug of choice.

I wasn't avoiding as much anymore in this new rebuilding chapter of my life. I felt proud of myself for not firing back when a pissed-off Cam, his voice filled with anger, would call me, send mean texts, or tell me how I was selfish for ruining our family and putting myself first. I just took it—*all* of it. I knew this side of Cam wasn't the real Cam. He was hurt, and I believed he'd eventually come around.

At least that's what I told myself—that things would get better, that it would only take time. Little did I know that in order for things to get better, they had to get a hell of a lot worse first.

Lessons I've Learned

It's Okay to Admit You're Not Okay

By the time I realized I was burnt out (physically and emotionally), it felt too late.

I was exhausted from building an empire and watching my marriage crumble at my feet. Of course, it *wasn't* too late; it's never too late to repair and transition into something else, but it certainly felt like it at the time.

I had been burning the candle at both ends for so long and had put tremendous pressure on myself to keep it together and not let anyone know I was unraveling. To the outside world, I was living a fairly glamorous life. But underneath the facade, I was a mess.

It wasn't until I started to pay attention to what I truly needed that I could start to nurture my personal life with as much care as

I had with my business. But that didn't come softly; I was forced into slowing down because I had hit a wall and couldn't keep going.

It's okay to take care of your needs. We aren't machines. It's impossible to keep going all the time without something falling out of balance.

Because we live in a world where it is very hard to disconnect, it will always be up to you to slow yourself down, put away the phone, put away the work, and take time to reflect.

No one can do that for you, so make sure you are really checking in with yourself.

When You're the Boss, You Get to Make Your Own Schedule

While running your own business is tough, one of the absolute best things about being an entrepreneur is not being enslaved to the nine-to-five mentality.

Yes, you have to consider your team and often work more hours, but you really do own your time.

How we structure our time is one of the most important things we do, both in and out of the office. When you truly realize you get to use your time as you see fit, a freedom emerges that is hard to ever give back.

Even if you don't own your own business, how can you more effectively use your time? How can you schedule time for yourself or your family? How can you stop looking at your phone for six hours a day and use that time to do something nourishing?

Most of us have heard before that we all have the same twenty-four hours in a day, whether you are a billionaire or unemployed. Pay more attention to the *fruit* of time spent, not the *focus* of time spent. Think about that extra hour you spent grinding through emails: Did the project really move forward? Did you feel better at the end? Or would an hour spent talking to your significant other or playing on the floor with your kids create the ROI you're really looking for?

I remember after my divorce, I felt like I had a lot more time: time to reflect, read, take more walks. I spent a lot of time alone since I didn't have my kids half the time. I used to walk to the top of my street and overlook LA and cry and listen to music and realize that I was going to have to trudge through an awful lot of darkness to get to the light. And I couldn't work my way out of this one or bury myself behind tasks. I was going to have to feel it, all of it, and use my time to heal.

It was ironic, because I still had the same amount of time in my day; I was just using it to focus on healing myself versus bitching about my relationship or hiding behind work.

It really is up to you how you use your time.

No Matter How Hard You Work, There Will Always Be More to Do

One day while I was a teenager working a shift at my parents' clothing shop, I snuck to the back office during some downtime and snatched a copy of *People* magazine. I sat back in my mom's office chair, feet propped up on the desk like I owned the place. Suddenly the door opened, and my dad walked in. I quickly sat up straight and stuffed the magazine behind my back, as if that were any less suspicious.

My dad just chuckled. "Alli, I don't care if you're looking at a magazine as long as you've done everything we've asked you to do."

The statement landed, full of importance.

My dad wanted me to work hard, but he wanted me to enjoy

life too. The same principle applies to you. If you are in the middle of building your business remember that there will always be more work; you will never, *ever* reach a place where all the work is done. We are not supposed to work all the time, and you're not being lazy when you choose other things.

Because of that, it's important to be able to turn it off, shut it down, and disconnect. Spend time with your loved ones, your friends, and even yourself. I wish I had found more balance back when I was working like a dog. I was so laser-focused on the business that I didn't allow for much else. At the time, I remember loving my work so much that it didn't occur to me I needed any kind of spiritual practice or break. I now see that I needed to reflect a bit more, soften up, and not have such a tight grip on things. But by constantly *doing*, I was avoiding *feeling*, which really kept me afloat at the time.

Probably, most honestly, I was avoiding some key feelings that needed expression. I loved certain feelings like excitement, appreciation, intensity, and satisfaction. I crafted my day and my life to have the most of those. It was the grief, sadness, incompetence, and isolation that I was running from. There's a principle in life: "Sunlight is said to be the best of disinfectants."[7] Because I didn't bring this darker side to the light, I was overcome by it.

Find activities that feel replenishing and nourishing; things that have nothing to do with work. So when you do get back at it, you are coming to the table with a full cup.

You can get *shit done* and still be focused on you.

What does fear look like?

Chapter Six

This May Surprise You

Being vulnerable allows you to face who you are
and what you need—in business and in life.

While my personal life was imploding, I was also facing another crisis: my mother was diagnosed with cancer and passed away.

Though I was profoundly grateful I got to say goodbye to her before she died and was beyond thankful I was with her as she crossed over, once she was gone, I also felt an odd sense of permission to let go and change.

As a result, I went into *go* mode yet again. In many ways, the process of watching my mom approach death was more challenging than her actual death. Mourning someone who is still alive is a hell of a thing. In the aftermath, I felt numb, so I threw myself into moving into the house of my dreams, with five thousand square feet and seven bedrooms. I felt I had finally made it—sort of. I moved in, got the kids settled, and then, just like that, it was back to business, which was booming.

It was back to "normal" life.

At the time, I couldn't see how much I was avoiding my mom's death or what a royal bitch I was being in general. Finally, I started seeing a new therapist who loosely diagnosed me with "situational depression." Apparently, I was avoiding the grief at all costs, so it kept coming out sideways. Cam confronted me about it, expressing that there had been a major shift in my emotional behavior and how I was treating him and others. Hearing his perception threw me off, and I started to understand that I was not addressing or coping with any of the changes that had happened the last few years.

It felt good to name it, but grief is a tricky thing: it continues to pop up in very strange and unpredictable ways. I threw myself even deeper into my business, keeping up appearances. *If I look okay, then I am okay,* I thought. I had pretty much staked my entire career on that philosophy. Keeping up the illusion is possibly our oldest survival technique.

. . . .

I knew that by throwing myself back into work, I was numbing out again, but work was my comfort zone. It felt safe. In the summer of 2018, after I appeared on the cover of *Inc.* magazine, my star was continuing to rise, even though I had lost so much personally. Just when I felt I was hanging on by a thread, I received an email from the showrunner at *Shark Tank*: "I was in an airport and saw you on the cover of *Inc.* and read your story. I think you'd be a great guest shark on *Shark Tank.*"

I read and reread the email several times. It felt like some kind of a prank. I mean, *me*? On *Shark Tank*?

Uh, yes please.

I had a couple of calls with the showrunner, and the next thing I knew, I was sitting at the Sony offices, meeting with more executives. They were vetting me, asking lots of questions to see if I could take the heat in the tank.

"Alli, you have to be comfortable jumping in and interrupting the other Sharks," they said, to which I responded, "You have no idea how good I am at interrupting."

Being assertive and extremely decisive is one of my superpowers. I wasn't scared to appear on the show—I love helping other entrepreneurs, and being on a national TV show doesn't suck either. But I did have a glaring insecurity, and that was around numbers. I wasn't good at calculating valuations and percentages in my head quickly. Because math isn't my strength, I worried about coming off looking less than impressive.

Hello, imposter syndrome! Quite frankly, I was afraid of looking stupid or making a fool out of myself. I wanted to appear smart and savvy.

Now, I want to be clear that not every entrepreneur is great in every area—that you can in fact run a successful business without the ability to compute valuations in your head. *And* it's A-OK, actually paramount, to hire people to fill in those gaps. But nonetheless, this was national TV, and I was nervous that people viewing would think I didn't know what I was doing.

Despite my reservations, I decided to do the show anyway. I was transparent about my insecurities, and the crew at *Shark Tank* were so cool about it and purposefully sat me next to Mark Cuban, who is a mathematical wizard and who graciously filled in some of the blanks for me.

I simply asked for help: it was available to me. It wasn't about looking a certain way: it was about being honest about my strengths and vocalizing my perceived weaknesses.

My biggest contribution to that show was my heart—being my authentic self and not being afraid to hold my ground among the other Sharks. I would speak up and give my real-world and hard-fought advice, and I loved every second of it.

As I loosened up, I realized that, though math might not be my strong suit, I did know what I was doing. I had scaled a thirty-five-dollar idea into a multimillion-dollar company, after all. I belonged in one of those chairs.

Filming *Shark Tank* was a very rewarding experience. We filmed from seven in the morning until nine at night, and the entire time, everyone was playful and lighthearted. There I was at one of the most popular shows on the air with people I aspired to be like; it was an extraordinary moment for me and I felt very accomplished.

. . . .

To the outside world, of course, it seemed my life was all good, but behind the scenes, I was still grieving the loss of my mother and my marriage. I felt like a complete mess, and it was one of those periods in life where every day was an emotional roller coaster—high highs and low lows that I couldn't explain. I would cry suddenly all the time and have no idea why. Also, I felt constantly anxious (mostly in my legs; anxiety is a tricky bastard).

On top of that, my son Grant had started to go off the rails. I knew something was very off with him, but I didn't want to see the depth of it because avoiding it was much easier. (I'm so embarrassed about that now.) I know I was selfish, and I regret a lot about that time. Grant had started smoking pot, and because of my very liberal upbringing and my parents' openness, I was exercising the same philosophy with my boys. However, as it turns out, my kiddos needed boundaries.

As hard as it is to admit now, because I was having such a

hard time taking care of my own emotions, I was having an even harder time wrapping my head around what my sons were going through. (Divorce is no joke.) During those first few months post-divorce, Cam and I were both trying to adjust to being single *and* single parents after sixteen years of partnership.

Our boys were put through the proverbial wringer during those months. At my house, I was usually pretty sad and cried a lot. I didn't do a good job of hiding what I was going through—mourning the death of my marriage and my mother. I can't imagine what that must have been like for the boys to witness their seemingly strong mama coming apart at the seams. At that time, I wasn't working much, but I did still have to fly to a handful of photo shoots that were absolutely brutal. I would hop from plane to plane, plastering on a smile for numerous articles, when I was only a shell of a human being. I am not looking for sympathy here, rather pointing out that there are times when we do what we have to do. However, the more I focused on showing up for others, the less I would show up for my own emotional well-being.

So, like anyone going through the depths of despair, I hopped on Instagram and DM'd a woman a friend had told me knew her shit when it came to matters of the heart (aka vulnerability). At this point, I was seeking help from everyone and anyone. You know how some people go inward when they are sad or depressed? Well, not me. As I mentioned earlier, I pretty much broke down to anyone in my path—I was downright desperate to feel better, be fixed, healed, whatever you want to call it! And of course, Instagram was a perfect outlet for said behavior. (Insert facepalm emoji.)

The woman I reached out to? Oh, you know, just Brené Brown. NBD. To be fair, this was several years ago, and she had not exploded into the public consciousness quite yet. My thumbs hovered over the keyboard on my phone. I wanted to send her a message and beg her for help. Maybe, just maybe, she would respond. I realized I had nothing to lose. I thought about typing something like, "I'm going through a little bit of a hard time (aka I feel like I am dying). You seem really well versed in this area. Would you help me?"

Little did I know that there was already a message waiting for me in another folder *from her*. This was also when I learned there's a whole section of hidden DM messages from people you don't follow. *What?* Apparently, when she saw me on the cover of *Inc.* (one of my career-defining moments), she shot me a message to congratulate me and invite me to a lunch she was throwing. *Which I missed!*

I was so raw when I messaged her back. My body and brain were telling each other that nothing in life was in harmony, but I had no idea where to begin unpacking my narrative. The best way I can put it, honestly, is that my insides were tangled, which felt contradictory to where I was seemingly supposed to be at this point in my life. After all, my professional dreams had all been realized beyond anything I could've imagined, and the divorce that I had been wanting and needing for so long had just been finalized.

So why was I still so fucked up and sad? It felt like a complete mystery to me.

When Brené and I started talking, she affirmed that the only real way to get through something like a divorce, death, or any hardship or trauma was to *go through* it. Make friends with it, even embrace it.

Ugh.

Turns out, I really needed two things: 1) time and 2) to fully acknowledge myself and my past so I could see exactly how I had played a role in everything that was falling apart around me, rather than scramble to find the next boyfriend, the next career milestone, or a new house or outfit. I had to face my shit, period.

The problem was I didn't *want* to go through. I wanted to skip over. Fast-forward, next! I wanted to go *around*. I was needy and beyond depressed. I missed my mom, and though I was confident in my divorce, I did not know how to be alone.

. . . .

After a lot of tough conversations, Brené connected me to Miles Adcox, the chairman of Onsite, a world-renowned emotional wellness retreat right outside of Nashville.

My heart had been broken open by my divorce, the demise of my co-parenting relationship with Cam, my mom's death, and my son Grant's downward spiral. Of course, I was not exempt from culpability in any of those areas, but instead of facing the heartbreak, I just kept looking toward an unrealistic sense of euphoria that came from new possibilities. As I discovered, that shit just wasn't working.

After one very weepy call with Miles, I decided to take Brené up on her advice to go to Onsite. Despite everything going on at home, I flew to Tennessee.

I arrived at Onsite a shell of myself. It was freezing outside—nothing but open land with horse stables, rolling hills, and beautifully appointed cabins with one main house for meetings and a mess hall that had the most delicious home-cooked food you could imagine. I had lost so much weight and needed that comfort food for so many reasons.

Though it was a place known to be frequented by celebrities, part of the genius of Onsite was not telling people who you were or what you did for work—no last names—because none of that mattered. What did matter was that people were there to listen and hold a safe space for each other, regardless of who you were or what was going on.

I spent six days slowly coming back to myself. With no phone and no one to be accountable to but myself, I really tuned in to how *I* felt and what *I* needed.

The break from reality was glorious.

I shared a cabin with a sweet girl who was really going through it too. We instantly became buds, shared our heartbreaking stories, and generally enjoyed each other's company. It was a little like summer camp—if summer camp was dark. Every day we got up, went to breakfast, did group meditation, and then we'd talk about what we experienced. From there, we broke into small therapy groups in which we spilled our guts to each other. It was humbling, vulnerable, hard, and utterly beautiful. Hearing about other people's experiences and hardships really put things in perspective. Watching others be honest with their sadness and trauma was a huge invitation for me to walk into the dark cave I had been so desperately avoiding.

After lunch, it was back to group, then a break for dinner and activities like campfires. One of my favorite guys in my therapy group was a very talented singer and guitar player who would strum away by the fire. It was so nice and comforting, a reminder of how community coming together can truly be healing. Every night, we'd sit by the fire and talk, and I was transported back to a simpler time in life. It was just what I needed.

Slowly, I began to let go of Alli the businesswoman, mom, and wife to become Alli the human who was just trying to figure it all out. For that week, my only job was to be myself, to let down my guard, be honest with those around me, and do whatever I needed to do to heal. I could say whatever I needed to say, cry when I needed to cry (which was *constantly*, Lord help me), and fess up to mistakes I had made. It was quite cathartic (sort of like writing this book). All the people there were *with* me. There was truly no judgment in that place—and boy, is that rare.

The biggest learning that week was *acceptance*. I had to accept that I couldn't hold onto things, even the good things, too tightly. I realized I wasn't going to feel better all at once, or all the time, and I also would not be depressed all the time. I would have to find a way to live in between. Don't we all?

Though my time at Onsite wasn't a cure-all, as so many of us hope that these breaks will be, it was a reset—a real opportunity to get perspective on my own shit because I was hearing about everyone else's lives too. I don't know about you, but when I sit back and hear heart-wrenching stories about child loss, incest, or sexual assault, it makes me see my own problems differently.

But it also showed me that we are all suffering in our own way, and it's important to have a safe space to land, process, and regroup.

My time at Onsite was a restoration of my humanity, where I could simply fall apart and still be held and seen. It was good to see people in that light again and to see myself. It's vital that we all carve out time to stop and take stock of our lives, even in the simplest moments.

When I checked out and they handed me back my phone, I didn't want it. I didn't want to leave and be on my own again. I didn't trust myself to bring this "new Alli" into my old world. At the airport, I stared at everyone, craned over their little glowing rectangular screens, and thought, *Why are we like this? How great would it be if we all just talked to each other about our feelings all day long and cried in each other's arms?* Okay, maybe that's a bit extreme, but you get the drift.

Onsite wasn't the magic bullet or shortcut to get through all the pain I wanted it to be, but as I waited in line to board the plane back home, I thought of Brené's words: "You have to feel and experience it all."

You have to go through it.

I came back home a little softer and a little more centered, feeling like I had really done some necessary work on myself.

Lessons I've Learned

We Take Our Shit With Us Wherever We Go

This is a lesson that would take me years to learn and embrace, so my hope is that this will resonate with you, wherever you are in your journey.

There's a famous quote: Wherever you go, there you are. It's true about our strengths, our power, and our gifts—but it's shocking to discover that it's also true about our weaknesses, our bullshit, and our selfish tendencies. Or at least it was for me.

The truth is, we all have baggage, and it's easy to keep creating more. If you are a person on this earth, then you carry the weight of all your stories, all your ups and downs, all your successes, all your fears, all your failures, and more. Baggage begets baggage. If you don't stop and address what's really going on, you'll multiply it. And if you don't watch it, others will know you by the weight of your baggage rather than the brilliance of your gifts. Really let that sink in.

I'm not asking you to see *if* you're broken. I *know* you are because we all are in some ways. You're human. We're all in conversations about what's wrong with ourselves, others, or the world at large. It's universal to be in these conversations. We can spend our lives trying to deny it or we can accept the fact that:

- We're not always who we want to be, and that's okay.
- People are not always who you want them to be, and that's okay.
- The world is not always as it should be, and that's okay.

Being willing to accept things as they are in the moment is the necessary—and only—starting point to healing, connecting, and transforming.

Accepting yourself, others, or your circumstances as they need to be in this moment allows us to enter in, be curious, connect, feel all the feels, want something new, take responsibility, and finally take that first step toward redemption.

As someone very close to me often says, when you look around and everything looks like shit, take your head out of your ass.

Burnout Is Real

People talk about burnout all the time, but I never knew what they were talking about.

I loved the breakneck speed of work, the impossible to-do list, the constant chaos of excitement and conflict. I wasn't burnt out. I was thriving, wasn't I?

Looking back, I can see that I was using work as the ultimate avoidance mechanism. When I was working, I was too busy to feel. It was safer to work than to be alone with myself and my thoughts. It was easier to build something than to look at myself in the mirror and decide if I even liked what I saw.

I don't think burnout is when life or work becomes too much.

I think it's when we've gone way past "too much" and are living in the warp speed of daily life. That's where burnout lives.

Burnout is a conversation. Burnout is a ready-made excuse for why we can't stop the madness, heal the pain, or fix the relationship. Burnout is what we do to avoid the pain, the struggles, hurting loved ones, or even yourself.

Though we can see what needs to be fixed, often we can't make things better. Why?

Because we're burnt the fuck out.

There's something to be said about when burnout actually hits, and you have no other choice but to face it. But why do we have to get to this place before we stop and really examine what's going on?

Wherever you are, whatever your path, stop often to assess if you're using work to avoid your feelings. That nightly glass of wine, that Netflix binge, that mindless scrolling? Those are also mechanisms to cover up our burnout, our feelings, and what we really need to face.

It's Not Only Okay to Show Vulnerability: It's Essential

So often in business, we try to appear as if we have all the answers.

We present ourselves as machines, churning and burning and hustling until we collapse in bed and then get up to do it all over again the next day. Every interview I had, every stage I spoke on, every Instagram story I posted wasn't about *me*; it was about my business. It was about getting shit done.

It wasn't about the divorce I was going through or the child I was worried about or the mother I'd lost. It wasn't about my depression, anxiety, or aching loneliness. Who would I be if I showed up to work and presented all my burdens to the world? Who would I be if I finally admitted I couldn't get it all done?

Again, that same question resurfaced: What would people think?

Well, here I am, laying it all out: being vulnerable *is* being human. Period. It's okay to admit when you can't get it all done, when shit is falling apart, and when you need a break. Though I love to work, life is not supposed to *be* all work. We cannot work all the time, and we cannot sacrifice the best parts of our lives in favor of a bottom line.

Look at yourself in the mirror and really figure out what it is you see. How do you feel? What do you need right now?

Start connecting who you really are with what you present out into the world—and you will find that when you show up, vulnerabilities and all, you start to connect in an entirely new way. You feel as though you have permission to be exactly who you are.

And that changes things.

Showing who you really are to the world empowers others to show up as their *true selves* too.

What have you never told anyone about yourself?

Chapter Seven

The Rise and Fall of a Great Idea

"You gotta know when to hold 'em, know when to fold 'em."[8]

*B*efore I tell you how it all ended, it's probably good to fill you in on how it all really began.

After bootstrapping the first few Drybar locations with our own money and from close family friends who invested around $1 million, it became clear that we needed to raise a lot more capital if we wanted to continue growing. We felt pressure to continue expanding rapidly, both to take advantage of the momentum and also to fend off would-be copycats.

We started receiving a ton of unsolicited offers to invest from random people, which, while flattering, was a bit overwhelming. We came close to taking a $5 million investment from a couple of private equity (PE) guys who had recently left a large, prestigious firm and were starting their own fund. (Thank goodness we didn't.)

Our close friend and lawyer, Jeff Williams, saved the day by writing us a *Jerry Maguire*–style memo, begging us not to do the deal because it just didn't feel right to him. He didn't completely trust the guys. He turned out to be *very right*, as we later learned they had a pretty bad reputation and, in retrospect, would have been a disaster to work with.

It was then that fate intervened.

Michael got a call from an amazing investment banker named Janica Lane, who was (at the time) at a small, boutique PE firm in San Francisco. Janica loved Drybar and wanted to help us. She held our hands through the process and gave us a crash course in raising capital and finding strategic equity partners.

To say there was so much we didn't know and understand is an understatement. We ended up hiring her and her partner, Brian Smith, to initiate a formal process to raise the capital we needed. But, most importantly, and I can't emphasize this enough, from the *right* partners.

It was such a breath of fresh air to be represented by true pros who knew how to properly position our business, evaluate the opportunity, and, most importantly, negotiate the best and right deal on our behalf. The type of potential investors we began meeting were night-and-day different from the people who were coming to us unsolicited. They were firms and people with real, relevant experience growing a business like ours. And the biggest decision we were left to make was who felt like the best people that we would get along with.

In my experience since then of talking to and working with various entrepreneurs at early stages of their growth, they often lose sight of this critical detail.

Taking a major investment from someone is like entering into a long-term, serious relationship. It isn't something that should be done with the person making the best offer.

You're going to work *extraordinarily* closely with these folks for a very long time. And it's not a relationship you can easily get out of if things aren't going great. So choosing carefully is really important. I could tell you horror stories about people who chose wrong, but that's a different book!

Once Brian and Janica ran the formal process of finding the right investors for Drybar, we encountered another challenge. The people we liked the most and collectively agreed added the most value and were the best partners were firms that had a larger minimum check size than we thought we wanted or needed to raise (which was around $5 million).

The people we liked best by far, Steve Berg and Janet Gurwitch, were at a firm called Castanea that wouldn't make investments smaller than $20 million, given the size of their fund. We were a bit smaller than their typical investment, but we all liked each other so much, we ended up figuring out a compromise that worked for both sides. They agreed to go down to $16 million, with $12 million going into the business and $4 million going toward secondary shares (buying equity from existing investors, such as Michael and myself and some of the aforementioned friends and family who invested early on).

Frankly, none of us before then even knew this was an option, but Steve wisely wanted Michael and me to take a little cash off the table at that stage so we wouldn't be as eager to sell the business down the road. For that, and many other reasons, Steve is a very smart man. (He has since started his own private equity firm called Stride Consumer. If you're ever lucky enough to have Steve interested in your business, we strongly recommend jumping at the opportunity.)

With investments in place and everything on track, Drybar

gained more success and notoriety. The business would soar for many years from all that capital, a great new CEO, the birth of a product line, and many more shops.

. . . .

After my mom passed away and Cam and I moved back to LA (pre-divorce) from a short and unsuccessful stint living in Orange County, I started losing my footing, emotionally speaking. As previously mentioned, I was avoiding grieving my mother, distracting myself with shopping, and decorating our extravagant new home in Studio City. My role at Drybar was also changing. At this point, we had hired so many people to do so much of what I was once doing that I started to feel lost in my own company. I was by no means being pushed out, but things were certainly changing.

I rolled with it. I was also starting to entertain outside opportunities mainly around the idea of TV shows and movies about my story (I know, so weird). At that time, and partially because of all of this, the board collectively decided to disengage me as a Drybar employee; rather, they put me on contract, which took months of negotiating my responsibilities and my salary. We came to an agreement, and it felt both unsettling and freeing.

During this time, we had found a cute little office not far from our new home in Studio City that would house the creative, marketing, and PR teams. John was worried that splitting up the teams would cause a rift in the company. He wanted everyone to stay together, but I was dying to get back to LA. We had so many shops opening and so much buzz in LA, and the two- to four-hour drive back and forth to the OC was too much—plus, I wanted my boys to grow up with a bit more diversity than Orange County could offer. So there I was. I had a new contract with Drybar, which felt weird. The office Cam and I shared was mostly his creative crew, so he took over that office, and as a result, I felt displaced. I started working from home, alone (pre-pandemic, this wasn't the norm), and I felt very isolated.

I began to feel lost. My identity, my shifting job, and the possibility of being on my own left me with questions: Who the fuck was I now, and where should I go? Once again, that depression gripped me by the throat. It was time for something else to give.

. . . .

The next year was a bit of a blur, but I was connected enough to know that all of us at Drybar felt ready to sell and move on. We'd been at it almost ten years, had opened over 150 locations, and had grown a massive product line. It felt like the right time to bow out. We also felt a bit of pressure from the many investors who had bet on us and were waiting patiently (some not so patiently) to see a return on their investment.

We hired different investment bankers to do a formal process and find the right, or best, buyer. While we initially imagined we would sell the entire company all at once, it quickly became clear to us that there were two very different buyers because we had two very different businesses, products, and shops.

Long story short, we ended up selling the *product* business first, to a publicly traded company called Helen of Troy. They are the folks behind HOT and Revlon tools, a bunch of major appliance brands, and many other brands you've probably seen at Target. They paid $255 million, which sounds pretty bonkers. (Before you get too excited, my portion of that was relatively tiny.)

Michael and I had personally taken money off the table every time we raised private equity money. Why, you ask? Michael got burned in the Yahoo! era—you know, back when the internet was becoming a thing. He worked for Yahoo! in its heyday when it was worth a lot on paper, but he didn't cash in early enough and didn't make nearly as much as his buddies who were set for life. He kicked himself for that and swore he'd never let that happen again. And he didn't.

He used to joke that the world could fall apart one day, and the business could go to shit; and all our hard work, blood, sweat, tears, and time would be worth nothing financially. I thought he was a little paranoid, but I trusted him nonetheless and wanted to learn from his mistakes. Who could have ever predicted the world would actually fall apart, and Drybar would be a hair away from having to declare bankruptcy?

It's vital for other founders out there to know this: selling the company was tremendously challenging and complicated, not to mention lengthy and tedious. I can tell you with 100 percent certainty it would not have gotten over the finish line without the help, persistence, and patience of my brother and one board member and our earliest investor, Steve Berg.

It took almost a year to close the deal; and each Friday *for months*, I would check in with Michael, who was working hard with the team on the details of the deal. We got very lucky to sell when we did because COVID was devastating to Drybar, particularly the shops. (Not a lot of women get their hair done during a global pandemic!) The shops that were extraordinarily profitable pre-COVID started losing *millions* of dollars every month. We were too big for government assistance (which is a whole separate book; don't even get me started).

Finally, we reached the point where we could no longer afford to keep the company running. We ended up selling all the stores—really giving them away to a group with deeper pockets who (hopefully) have enough staying power to get Drybar back to its pre-COVID glory.

. . . .

Instead of running Drybar, I would now be rooting from afar for this thing I had built. It felt like giving away a limb and would prove to be a long spiritual journey to make peace with the fact that Drybar was no longer my baby.

It's such an odd feeling to no longer be at the helm of this company. I built Drybar with my family, and I dedicated my whole heart and life to it—but that's also the price of doing business, especially *big* business. We've all heard stories of companies growing so large that the founder(s) can become irrelevant. Now that person was *me*. It's just the way it goes.

A few years back, someone asked me if I was okay with having sold my company. My initial response was, "Yes, 100 percent," but then he asked me if I was *spiritually* okay. Again my response was an emphatic *yes*. But wait a second. Was I?

That question lingered. And truth be told, I still struggle sometimes because I truly love what we built and how we serve so many women and have become a daily pick-me-up in so many people's lives. It's such a beautiful company that will always be part of my legacy.

However, while my personal identity was so tightly wrapped up in Drybar, all good things must come to an end. Things change . . . in fact, everything changes and evolves, and I am truly okay with that. Not only did it open hundreds of doors and opportunities for me and others, it also taught me so many life lessons and gave me a pretty incredible life all around.

I'm deeply grateful for all of it. Even for the ending, as I truly believe it has been a humbling experience for me.

One that took my life in an entirely new direction.

Lessons I've Learned

Before You Raise Money, Explore Your Options

There are many different ways to raise money. I strongly urge you to exhaust as many options and possibilities as you can when setting out to raise funds. When we were raising money for Drybar, we had a lot of really disappointing meetings with men in suits (as I like to call them) who just didn't get me or us. They didn't understand our mission and couldn't understand why we weren't essentially taking advantage of the hundreds of women who were coming to Drybar daily.

"Why don't you sell makeup or do lashes or manicures?" they asked.

It was a fair question, and while I understood the desire to make as much money as possible, money wasn't *ever* the main driver for me. The purity of the *experience* was the holy grail. I was determined to keep hair, specifically blowouts, at the forefront of what we did. That turned off a lot of potential investors. Fair enough, and no thanks.

I also urge you to be as discerning as you can and as aligned with potential investors as humanly possible. Like a marriage, this is a massive commitment and not to be rushed, no matter how tempting the offer is.

Don't just take a big check. Instead, make sure whomever you allow to invest in your baby is spiritually aligned with you long-term. Having a shared vision is critical to your success and happiness.

Show Me the Money

When seeking investors, talk to as many people as you can—friends, family, colleagues, even strangers you meet at events. You'll be shocked how many potential investors are just a friend away. The world is incredibly small.

I'm a big believer in manifesting what you want. I can't remember a time where I put out a request to the universe that wasn't fulfilled. That may be a bit too woo-woo for some of you, but I am telling you there is a lot of power in speaking what you want into existence. It works.

Over the years, I have gotten more and more comfortable saying what I really need or want. Talking to people in a social setting about where your business is or what you're looking for can yield big results.

Speaking of, *always* go to events! So many deals are born there. As somewhat of an introvert myself, I'd often rather be in my bed watching my favorite show by 8 p.m., but going to an event or dinner pays off in so many ways. I have developed so many friendships and business relationships simply by showing up and being open to meeting new people.

When Someone Gives You Their Money, You Have to Play by Their Rules

So many people want an investable business.

It means it's worthy, right? It means someone is willing to take a risk on your business (and you) because they believe in what you're selling. To secure money can be an awesome thing, but it also comes with an incredible responsibility.

Every investment comes with strings; some good, some bad. When you open your doors to investors, you are playing on a new field, with new rules. (I learned this lesson quickly.)

It's vital to understand the ins and outs of said investment up front. Are you really ready for it? Will it add to the value of your business? Will it allow you to grow? Will it help scale the business? Or will it add more risk and responsibility? Will it add pressure before you're ready?

Sometimes, we are so eager to grow that we don't stop to ask ourselves if we're *really* ready. If the business is really ready. Before you accept money, talk to other business owners who've received an investment. Crack into their experiences and what they wish they would have known.

What's right for others might not be right for you; make sure to do your due diligence ahead of time.

It's all about the timing.

Money isn't the answer to all your problems: *you* are the answer to all your problems.

How would you live your life if there were no consequences?

Part Three

Embrace
Your Mess

Chapter Eight

The Hardest
Job of All

Parenting is a balancing act between building a solid
foundation and then watching it all crumble.

*B*efore we go any further, I want to talk about my teenage son Grant.

While this chapter focuses on Grant, who is eighteen, my other son, Kit, who is sixteen, is much more private and would respectfully like to be left out of this book.

But I want to take a moment to acknowledge the amazing kid Kit is. When he was younger, our relationship was very strained, and I wasn't the best mom. I was pretty impatient and had very little room for him. I won't go into great detail, but when the shit hit the fan with Grant, Kit (who was just eleven at the time) really matured and said something to me I'll never forget: "I know how much you guys are dealing with around Grant, so I want it to be easier for you."

Up until that point, Kit had been very argumentative; the kind of kid you couldn't teach anything to. I said black; he said white. He was stubborn and strong-willed and challenged us at every turn.

The time Grant spent away from us would prove to be a blessing in disguise for my relationship with Kit. As the second child, he didn't really ever have alone time with me or Cam, so while Grant was in treatment, Kit and I grew much closer and have the best relationship now, which I am deeply grateful for.

That being said, my hope here is that Grant's story can help a lot of struggling youth and parents, so this is my focus for this chapter. (If you're not a working parent, then feel free to skip to the next chapter!)

......................:....

During my divorce, Grant was going through some dark shit. We all were, but unbeknownst to me, he had long been collecting small traumas from myriad experiences: from moving a lot when he was young, which meant he was never able to establish a solid friend group; from his severe acne, which messed with his self-confidence and made him uncomfortable in his own skin; and from being lauded as "the golden child" while his brother wreaked havoc and was always in trouble, which put Grant under immense pressure. It seemed everything in him boiled to the surface all at once, about the same time as my issues did for me. Good times.

The grief, the move, and finding new schools all at once was *a lot*, and I didn't even consider the traumatic impact it had on the boys. It was already a precarious time for Grant, who was in the throes of puberty and the new kid at a new school, grieving his grandmother's death, and adjusting to a whole new environment. *Oy.*

Right before Cam and I separated, Grant started experimenting with drugs. It began with smoking weed, which honestly, I was okay with in small doses, as long as he kept up his grades. Like many teenagers, he had a lot on his plate and found some relief in the temporary escape pot provided. That relief would become a huge crutch for him to escape from his internal pain.

Grant and I always had a beautiful bond and had been able to talk openly and with ease about everything under the sun—but I think the separation, coupled with watching his mom fall apart right before his eyes, was the final straw for him. Of course, none of us could see this while we were living it, but boy, is it clear as day now. I was so consumed with my own sadness and failure that I was hardly paying attention to what was going on with my kids. I had lost a lot of my zest for life, and my depression was palpable. While I remember trying to hide this (somewhat) from my kids, they undoubtedly saw through that and straight into my pain.

I was a shell of myself during this phase, and like Grant, I was just trying to survive; we all were. Cam was dealing with his pain in a very different way than I did, but that's not my story to tell. As embarrassing as this is, we didn't really notice when Grant's pot smoking started to get out of control (he was consuming so much that later, a therapist would suggest a "pot schedule" just to taper off). Ugh, I still hold a lot of guilt and shame around not paying close enough attention to him.

He was self-medicating (a term I only learned once Grant began treatment). He wanted to feel better. He was lost and sad, and he had a girlfriend who caused him a great deal of upheaval and pain, but he also couldn't quite articulate what troubled him—all of which made it hard to understand how to help him. It was incredibly frustrating for all of us.

Grant eventually started chasing pot with other drugs. And he became so dependent on pot that he brought it to school and, of course, got kicked out as a result.

Things just kept getting worse and I didn't know how to reach Grant or myself, for that matter. The four of us, while all on our own journeys, were so very lost and disconnected. I now know it's so hard to help anyone else when you haven't helped yourself (like the oxygen mask instructions flight attendants give you on the plane). I didn't know how to help him, but I know I played a big part in the unraveling. When I tried to talk to Grant about how harmful pot was, I was coming from a very dogmatic place of, "I know more than you, Grant, so just listen to me, dammit!" That's what fear sounds like. I realize now that I was so out of touch with my own fear that I resorted to wanting or needing to be right. I was trying to fix him so we could get on with it, hurrying the process to save me from challenges he needed to face.

I also later learned that my know-it-all attitude didn't work. Grant and I used to get in such terrible fights on our morning drive to school where I would come at him with a lot of anger and would essentially shame him by telling him things like, "If you don't get your act together and stop smoking pot, you're never going to do anything great with your life." Man, my own pride that hindered my learning back then still makes it hard to write this and remember how unhinged and ridiculous I was. It's like that old saying: "Hurt people hurt people."

I'll never forget the moment Grant revealed all the cuts on his wrists. The summer before he was in ninth grade, I picked him up from summer football practice, and the four of us—me, Kit, Grant, and Cam—went to dinner. This was a big deal since things were still pretty shaky with me and Cam at the time. We were at a Greek restaurant on Ventura Boulevard in Sherman Oaks when, in a fit of rage, Grant rolled up the sleeves of his oversized sweatshirt, peeled off the football tape around his wrists, and revealed something that would haunt me for years. I gasped at the dozens of cuts along his tender flesh, not daring to imagine what would happen if he had pressed just a little harder. I felt ill, beside myself with confusion, pain, and sadness. That's when we knew we were in real trouble. It was a terrifying discovery, and I felt panicked.

I had *zero* experience with cutting. I didn't know anyone who had ever done it, and I didn't understand why he was doing it—inflicting serious harm to himself. *Is it a suicide attempt? Does he want to die? Do we need to take him to a psych ward?* I kept thinking I was the worst parent. I would later learn it was a deep cry for help. And that I had made a lot of parenting mistakes.

Grant was visibly troubled, and most of our conversations around that time involved us trying to understand what the hell was going on with our kid. My anger and disapproval of what he was doing only made him retreat even more. I eventually learned that teenagers like to do the exact opposite of what you ask or tell them to do. (Years later, Grant would explain that to me.)

He would get so mad at us and say things like, "You don't understand!" and "Why aren't you helping me?" We were so baffled by this.

"Helping you with what?" we asked. "You won't tell us what's wrong." We asked him what was going on. We begged him to let us in, to open up. But he wouldn't. He said he *couldn't*, even though he wanted to. He himself did not understand or have the language to explain his pain. None of us had the language back then to deal with any of this. It was so hard to watch my baby suffer so much—this was a whole new level of pain I'd never experienced. He was drowning in traumas he could not name.

. . . .

One night, when Grant was staying at Cam's house, I came over to try to connect with him and get him off the couch and into some fresh air. We went on a walk, and he ran away from me. I ran after him, but he'd already vanished. More panic and anxiety set in. Anxiety at this level and a shit ton of crying were becoming a pretty normal state for me. I ran back to Cam's house, waiting desperately for the phone to ring and praying Grant would show up at the door—*wrong*. When it was nearing midnight, I said to Cam, "I can't take it. I'm calling the police." He thought I was overreacting, but I felt so powerless and just had to do something.

After I called the police, I also called my neighbors and asked them if they had seen anyone come into my house, thinking maybe Grant had gone to my house instead of Cam's. They hadn't seen anyone. Desperate, I asked them if they would be willing to go in and see if by chance Grant was there.

Sure enough, Grant was at my house, and my neighbors said the house reeked of pot. I immediately called the police to explain we had found him, and they didn't need to come. But because he was a minor, they said they now *had* to come. It was protocol apparently. I felt the urge to warn Grant (protect him like always).

I just barely made it in the door of my house moments before the cops did. The house was basically a hotbox. Grant had found the pot I confiscated and smoked it. To his credit, he was cleaning his room when I got there. In the midst of all this, he was still trying to please me in his own way. The cops arrived, which was a bit scary for all of us. What were they going to think of the marijuana smell? For a moment, I wondered if we would all go to jail.

The officers were incredibly kind. They had a good chat with Grant alone and then proceeded to tell us, "If you don't put him in some sort of program, we're going to have to take him in."

"I'm sorry, what?" I said. "You can't just take my kid."

Suddenly, this wasn't just a marijuana problem or a phase of teenage rebellion. This was *serious*. Grant needed help we were not equipped to give him. Cam and I frantically tried to come up with a plan, a way to help our son.

. . . .

After some research, we found Polaris Teen Center, a treatment center for teens. Cam called the facility and explained the situation we were facing and how we were desperate for help. Helping Grant was all that mattered; so despite the shocking price tag, Cam and I decided to send him, not knowing what was ahead of us. Even though this particular program was meant to only be four to six months, I remember Cam saying to me, "This is just the beginning. We have a long, long road ahead of us." I didn't want to believe him, but deep down, I knew he was right.

When we told Grant, he naturally freaked out. He didn't want to leave his girlfriend, his pot, or his lifestyle. He shut down. It was as sad as you can imagine. I didn't want to take him to rehab; I just wanted things to go back to normal. Well, not really—my new normal had become unsustainable—but I sure didn't want what was behind this door. The pain and shame were unbearable. But finally, after some negotiating and convincing, Grant reluctantly agreed to go. I believe that on some level he wanted the help, and while he wasn't willing to admit it then, he eventually thanked us years later.

When we pulled up to a gorgeous, gigantic house in the Valley, I relaxed a little. *Maybe this won't be so bad,* I thought. Grant was silent.

We didn't know what to expect when we walked in, but everyone was kind and welcoming. They checked him in and asked us tons of questions. It was clear Grant was very angry and upset and didn't want to be there. As it was nearing time for us to leave, he locked himself in the bathroom. We tried to get him to come out, but he wouldn't.

The director told us to leave. I was hysterical, just beside

145

myself. I was so torn up inside. I knew this was a good thing for Grant, a place that could potentially help him, but the thought of leaving him there gutted me. I was also scared Grant would think we were abandoning him. Would he ever forgive me? I knew we wouldn't be able to see him for a couple of weeks, and it was important to me to say goodbye to him. I needed, in a very codependent and unhealthy way, for *him* to make *me* feel better about *my* decision. That wasn't happening, however. This would be the beginning of my healing too.

Because of the cutting issue and the potential suicide ideation, Grant was put on a twenty-four-hour watch. I was devastated. It was as dark a time as I can ever remember. I left Polaris feeling so alone.

My depression grew.

We had a couple of calls with Grant, which were pretty rough. He lashed out at me a lot. He told me he hated me. I knew it was his anger speaking, but I now understand he *was* angry at me for not slowing down and really listening to him when he needed it most. I wish I had started working on myself more then, but I was caught in a victim mentality. I thought all this stuff with Grant was happening to *me*. I was way too concerned with myself. It would take me a very long time to come out of this stage of victimhood (a place I still visit from time to time).

．．．．．．．．．．．．．．．．．．．．．．．．

After Grant had been there a couple of months, we were told Polaris wasn't the right place for him, but he wasn't ready to come home. *Well, shit,* I thought. *What now?*

"I really want him to come home," I insisted (focused on *me* again!). I worried that they just wanted to make more money or

146

send him to a place that was even more expensive. But I eventually realized I was operating from my own wants and fears, not what was best for Grant.

So we enlisted help from a trusted friend, a consultant of sorts, to help us navigate what would span almost two years and three different treatment centers. We found a therapeutic wilderness program in Utah called Evoke Therapy Programs, where kids learned to live off the land, engaged in group therapy, camped in the wilderness, worked on accountability letters (aka "how you messed me up letters" to parents—more good times), learned to make campfires, and lived an overall simpler life. It was a really beautiful experience; one I think every human should be required to go through.

Though that time apart from him was incredibly hard for me, Grant was starting to shift. He was doing the work when a lot of the kids in the program were just phoning it in so they could go home. Cam and I spent one weekend at Evoke and witnessed our beautiful boy in a whole new light. He was essentially living off the land, easily whipping up a fire, preparing his own food and ours. He even whittled me a ring and a spoon made out of wood. He had grown so much. I was overcome with pride watching him blossom and all his hard work pay off. He was coming home to himself, but he still wasn't ready to come home to *us*.

When he successfully finished Evoke, we were warned that he couldn't just be tossed back into his same old environment, so we sent him to a therapeutic boarding school called Crossroads to help him reacclimate to everyday life. The school was designed to help kids discover other things they loved, like skateboarding, surfing, and mountain biking. And Grant actually wanted to go—well, at least he didn't put up a fight about going. I think he knew he wasn't quite ready to come home.

All the way through, Grant was doing the work. He says he learned he was just as troubled, and just as capable, as anyone else, and that there is always more learning to do. He no longer wanted to be put on a pedestal. He just wanted to be recognized for exactly who he was. He grew so much and became the most awe-inspiring version of himself.

. . . .

While Grant was healing, I was healing too. Looking back, I wish I had been more curious about what Grant was going through instead of simply feeling like I had to rush to fix him. I wish I had asked him more questions and been a safer place for him to land.

However, I knew that in order to do that going forward, I had to work on healing myself too. Slowly, I started to come out of my depression. I was feeling a bit of rebirth, like I had just crawled out of a wicked storm and could see the light again. I'd been mourning (a term I was unwilling to embrace for a very long time) the loss of my old life and the person I used to be, as well as my life partner. Though it took time for me to realize it, there was a big hole left in the wake of my divorce. Once I named it, I began to come to terms with it.

I realized I had been chasing a new relationship out of fear of being alone; being okay with singleness would be the key to my ultimate happiness.

I decided to give myself the time I needed to rediscover who I was on my own—to fall apart, build myself back up, become a better mama, and create space for who I wanted to be in the next chapter of my life. Because, really, *who* was I now? What did I even like? What did I truly want?

Grant told me one of his biggest takeaways from treatment was the ability to take a hard look at himself—to see where he's going from an outside perspective and choose whether or not it's what he wants from life. It gave him a sense of awareness. And, in a way, I was gaining this kind of awareness too.

I began to realize that the depression I experienced during my separation from Cam was a gift. Had my life not completely fallen apart, I wouldn't have been able to put it back together and discover who I really wanted to be.

Yes, my business and my day-to-day responsibilities had shifted. Yes, I'd lost my identity. Yes, every single thing in my life had changed; and yet, because of that change, I had softened. I was becoming better, more empowered, more open. I began to love the new me.

I realized that from time to time, life simply blows up. What we experience when it happens isn't regression but grief. I had been grieving. I finally got the memo that it was important to feel those feelings—to understand them, acknowledge them, and then let them go.

Once I did that, I decided I wanted to stand on my own two feet for a while.

. . . .

I'd be remiss if I didn't update you on Grant. He came home from treatment toward the end of his sophomore year and took some time trying to find his way through eleventh grade. But he stayed sober and was rediscovering this new version of himself, just like I was.

He eventually decided to go back to playing football for his senior year and absolutely soared. He worked his ass off to become a starter and has accepted a partial scholarship to play football at Denison University in Granville, Ohio (after only playing high school football for one year!).

I can't put into words the pride I have for this kid, not just for all he's achieved but for *how* he got there.

Lessons I've Learned

Address Your Own Wants and Needs

"What would you do differently if you could go back?" I never liked this question, but I have been asked it a ton of times.

I like to think that I wouldn't really change anything, but because the question has been posed to me so often, I have reluctantly given it more thought. The answer that comes up for me most is around my kids.

Raising kids is so damn hard. If you know, you know. While I think it is absolutely the greatest love there is, parenting is also the most challenging journey you will ever take. Particularly, taking care of your own needs as a working parent feels impossible. I often—almost always, in fact—put my work and my kids' needs in front of my own needs. But I've come to see that, though we parents make that vital commitment to love and care for our children first, we must enjoy and thrive in our own lives too.

I felt this intensely as I boarded the figurative Drybar rocket ship. I wondered anxiously whether I was a bad parent, or less dedicated to my children, for wanting to build something for myself. But I am here to tell you—I was not, and neither are you.

You are not a bad parent for wanting and striving to have the best of both worlds. I sincerely wish I hadn't spent so much time worrying about falling short.

But how do we do it? How do we balance *our* needs and our *kids'* needs? Beats me.

Just kidding. The fact is that it's personal to each parent. For me, having balanced conversations with my kids about my life and the work I was doing while also talking about their lives and what was important to them helped a lot. I sought to understand what I needed to be there for in their lives and what was not a big deal to them. Yes, my boys hemmed and hawed when I had to leave town for days at a time, but I talked to them about how much I loved what I was doing and how pursuing my dreams made me a better, more satisfied mama. While this was harder for them to comprehend when they were young, it did eventually sink in. And I know they get it and appreciate it now.

Anytime I tell Grant how proud I am of him, he responds, "I'm proud of you, too, Mom."

Cue the tears.

Stop Feeling Guilty for Working

I was very fortunate to have my mom around to watch my boys when I was working and traveling like crazy. But this didn't always alleviate the tremendous guilt that weighed on me both as a professional *and* a mom.

When I was at work, I felt guilty for not being at home. When I was at home, I felt guilty for not being at work. Not exactly the healthiest model.

I strongly encourage you to spare yourself this unnecessary and unneeded guilt. It serves absolutely no purpose. It does nothing except to demonstrate the painful reality that you're not a superhero. Somehow that guilt has a very sneaky "trade" baked into it. If I feel guilt, like I'm doing something wrong, then I don't have to look at the shame, or the deeper fear that I'm not enough. If I beat myself up about it, it also is a way to protect myself from the feedback of others. If I already feel bad, then you have no right to point out what I'm doing wrong, dammit! Looking back, I now know this to be true.

If you are a working mother, you will find yourself in this position, period. You can read all the books, try to strike a balance, and invite in all the support and help you need—but inevitably, you will always feel as if you are not doing enough.

One of the most helpful tools I've found is simply being present. It's not about the amount of time you're at work or at home; it's about the *quality* of that time. When I am with my kids, I am fully there—not mindlessly scrolling on my phone or answering emails (mostly—let one who is without sin cast the first stone, am I right?). When I'm at work, I'm at work, trusting that my children are okay.

No matter who you are or what your situation is, you are never going to be in the perfect position. There will always be a juggling act because that's life.

So learn that juggling is simply part of the crazy ride of life. Enjoy your time. Stay present.

Let go of the guilt.

Your Kids Do Not Belong to You

I remember when I had Grant, my whole world changed.

For the first time in as long as I could remember, I felt fully on purpose. I loved this little boy with my entire being, and I couldn't imagine a world in which he didn't come to me with his problems, his joys, his fears, or his tears.

As Grant grew, so did his independence. It's one of the biggest conundrums of parenting: we sacrifice our bodies, our sleep, and sometimes our relationships for these pivotal years most of our children don't even remember. We make endless mistakes (and memories) and hope, by the time we send them out into the world, that we have given them enough of a foundation to survive. We feel their pain. Their mistakes are our mistakes. Worry becomes a full-time job.

But here's the rub: as much as I love my children, they are not mine. They came through me, but they are living their *own* experience, out in the world. And despite this unpopular opinion, I really don't know what's best for them; they do. It's my job to guide them and expose them to as much as I can emotionally and spiritually, which doesn't always mean rainbows and sunshine. I believe kids need to experience a certain amount of adversity, tough times, and grit before they head out into the world alone.

The biggest and most tangible lesson I learned when Grant was going through rehab was to get a lot more curious and listen even more. I naively thought that, with all my years of wisdom (ha!), my advice would somehow convince him to stop smoking pot and to make different decisions. Wrong. In fact, it made him go in the exact opposite direction.

Back then, I wasn't willing to listen to Grant because I knew I was right and believed I was smarter. Wrong again. I needed to *hear* my son; I needed to accept and meet him where he was. He needed me to listen to him and support him. That wasn't all he needed, but it was a start.

In my experience, the worst thing we can do as parents is demand our kids be a certain way or be someone they aren't. Instead, try to learn more about them, work to get to know them, and give them space to come to you when they are ready.

It is imperative that we set our children up to thrive, but their choices, decisions, successes, and failures are ultimately theirs—not yours.

They are on their own journey, just as we are.

Try *listening* instead of lecturing; it goes a long way.

What did you enjoy doing the most as a child?

Chapter Nine

When Life Gives You Lemons, Go Buy Some Fucking Limes

Sometimes the second time's a charm.

After the business sold and Grant was starting to turn a corner, I was a free agent in every way. I figured I *finally* had space in my life to think about love again.

I was forty-something and nearly divorced, and it seemed the only options I had were to get on a dating app and pray to the love gods to find someone. Shopping for men—that sounds fun, doesn't it? Wrong.

I imagined I would be some sort of serial dater. Let me explain. Most (or all) of my adult relationships, I'd grown bored—emotionally and sexually—at around the six-month mark. I assumed this was normal for everyone, but to be honest, I don't think I actually thought about it much back then.

After being married for sixteen years, the idea of dating several boyfriends until I got bored seemed like a wonderful plan at the time. I didn't want to get married again. I would just date until the initial fun wore off, and then I would meet someone new. No muss, no fuss.

Being footloose and fancy-free was fun for a while (like, *really* fun, as I dated a few guys much younger than I was), but I came to realize that I really wanted a partner, and I wanted to find a real relationship.

And dating, as it turned out, sucked.

Dating at forty-five wasn't like dating at twenty-five. It was way more complicated. *Everyone* had baggage, including me. It felt next to impossible to find someone whose life could merge with mine. It was hard to keep the conversation fun and flirty with my divorce, the added pressure of Grant in rehab, and creeping out of my depression. To put it mildly, I was worried that I might not meet anyone. *Ever.* I couldn't stop picturing my life alone. (With cats. Lots and lots of cats.)

My mind flashed to my own parents after their divorce. Though my mother briefly dated other men before she died at sixty-five, she never met another serious partner; and my father has spent the last twentyish years pretty much single as well. I didn't want that to be my story too. I was convinced I had a very short window to meet someone, and the endless stream of bad dates was clashing with my newfound sense of confidence.

Here I was, looking pretty good, feeling better than ever, and at the peak of my career, yet feeling manic and scrambling around to find a new person. I felt successful and accomplished, with so many professional opportunities coming my way—so love couldn't be far behind, right?

As it turned out, love wouldn't show up until I was sincerely and honestly A-OK on my own, really enjoying my life and my boys, and no longer sitting in that desire to go find someone. What's that old expression? When you're not looking, love appears.

After my divorce, I started thinking seriously about all the qualities I wanted in a man. I even made a list. (Yup, manifest that shit, y'all.) I remembered the feeling I had when we raised our first tranche of private equity money at Drybar (about $25 million) and formed an official board. I was suddenly surrounded by a lot of assertive, direct, and impressive businessmen. I liked it. I liked the strength and confidence these men brought to the table. It was something I had never been exposed to. I'd always gone for the metrosexual, super creative type, but now, I longed for a different kind of man.

I was learning I was now, later in life, a completely different person, attracted to a completely different type of man. I wanted someone strong and assertive but not threatened by my success.

Finding a man like that turned out to be like hunting for a damn unicorn.

I slowly started to tire from the dating scene. It was exhausting and *not* helping me on my journey to elevate my mental health. But, as you may have picked up by now, I am pretty driven when I get my mind set on something, and I'm proud of this quality. So I pushed forward on the dating apps, not really knowing where else to turn.

. . . .

Before the divorce, Michael and I had started our own podcast, *Raising the Bar*, interviewing fellow entrepreneurs. We talked about the ups and downs of starting, growing, and scaling a business. The show received an abundance of guest pitches, but one in particular would prove to be a complete life-changer for me.

Her name was Talia Goldstein, and she had a matchmaking business called Three Day Rule. The Monday before she came on the show, I'd literally just broken up with someone. I should note that private matchmakers approached me when my split went public, but they were insanely expensive—like one hundred thousand dollars expensive. I just couldn't get on board with spending that kind of money.

So I was kind of skeptical of Talia. I didn't know much about who she was or what set her matchmaking service apart, but I still thought she could be an entrepreneur of interest to our podcast audience. Plus, I can't deny that there was a part of me that wanted to hear an expert explain how to find a soulmate. I mean, who doesn't want to know how to do that?

We started off talking about her time at E! when she'd set up a rebellious tattooed guy with a preppy girl from the accounting department. Even though it had been a seemingly unlikely match, she intuited it would work perfectly, confident in her abilities to set up people who on paper might not appear to be a great fit.

Then she said something that really stuck with me: "We prioritize so many different services and people in our lives, right? We pay for trainers, therapists, personal financial advisers, and all the different things that we do. Great, so why don't we prioritize love on the same level and pay for it?"

Holy shit. Maybe she had a point. People went to therapy to help solve their inner conflicts, talk about their lives, and heal. Hell, people paid me to do their hair, even though, theoretically, they could learn how to do it themselves. Why were we so quick to pay other people to handle other parts of our lives, but not our love lives?

Despite my initial hesitations, after listening to Talia, I was all in.

. . . .

Talia's premise was simple: you get set up with three different potential matches by a matchmaker. They took the time to scout out the guys, then they went on a "first date" on your behalf.

(Hallelujah!) My matchmaker happened to be a family and marriage counselor, so I trusted her to foresee how a relationship might play out.

My first match was with a semifamous actor—and boy, did that fizzle quickly. Then they found me a guy in San Francisco, but the distance made connecting too challenging for me to be willing to put in the effort. Next.

I was starting to lose faith in this whole matchmaking thing. Did people really find love this way?

Then one fateful night, I was on a date with a guy I'd met through a popular LA dating app called Raya. We were at a swanky new restaurant downtown, flirting and chatting away. The wine was flowing, and I was genuinely enjoying myself, when I got a text from match number three.

"Hey, my name is Adrian," the text said. "Sorry for the late message. I've been burning the midnight oil, but I got your information from Three Day Rule and would love to connect."

I felt a flutter of excitement but pocketed my phone since I was already on a great date. The next morning, I texted him back, which set in motion a flurry of texts. That night, while I was on the way to meet my son Kit for dinner, Adrian called me out of the blue—like, *on the phone.* My initial thought was, *What is happening? We're on a text-only basis,* but I answered anyway.

"Why are you calling me?" I asked bluntly.

"It's how phones work," he replied.

I smiled—confidence *and* wry humor, both of which I liked. I laughed, we spoke for a minute, and then Kit slammed into my window, scaring me, as children so often do. I told Adrian I'd call him back later.

I could barely wait to talk to him again, and I called him

when I got home. We talked until five the next morning. We told each other so much about ourselves, and I was enamored by him. He was smart, kind, loving—and he seemed to instantly understand me.

During one of our marathon conversations, he said, "I bet it's really hard for you to date. Most guys who are more successful than you are probably pretty checked out emotionally. If they are less successful than you, they are probably intimidated. My guess, Alli, is that you need someone secure enough to let you be as big as you are and also sensitive enough to give you the space to be as small as you need to be and a safe place to land."

. . . .

I had to leave for a trip to New York and San Francisco the next day. While I was on the road, we continued to talk, text, and FaceTime. We couldn't get enough of each other. We decided meeting was definitely the next step. He offered to pick me up at the airport when I returned from my trip. Most people gasped at this gesture, but I thought it was romantic.

My thoughts ran in circles the entire flight. The sensation of meeting a person for the first time—someone who I felt oddly connected to already—was disorienting and exhilarating.

I made sure to hit the ladies' room to brush my teeth and spruce up, as I instinctively knew this was going to be a very important first meeting. And it was. When I walked out of JetSuiteX (look it up; it's awesome), there he was, waiting for me with an unassuming smile. He took my suitcase, and just like that, I was captivated.

Without a word, he very smoothly put his hand on my knee. It was the first time we had ever touched, but it felt so natural.

"You're touching me," I said.

"Yup," he joked, as if it was nothing. "How was your flight?"

Adrian proved himself to be charming, assertive, and strong.

That first night, we shared a four-hour dinner in a quaint little Italian restaurant on Ventura Boulevard in Studio City. We both told our stories of the demise of our previous failed marriages.

I sensed he had experienced a profound internal shift, and I could feel integrity emanating from him. At that time, Grant was still in rehab and I was in the middle of my own mess, trying to make sense of it.

I carried a lot of shame about having a kid in rehab. I truly thought I must be a pretty shitty mom and wondered who would want to be with someone like me who had a kid in rehab. Serious shame loomed, so that lie obsessively played in my head. But to my delight, Adrian didn't judge me at all. He was very open and would turn out to be one of the biggest advocates for my son.

In the span of a couple of hours, we both laid it all out: our mistakes, regrets, and intentions. He wanted me to know who he was and who he wanted to become.

. . . .

When he brought me home, I gave him the tour of my bachelorette pad, which I was very proud of. Nestled in the Hollywood Hills up Lookout Mountain in Laurel Canyon, it was a spot I'd always dreamed of having. A place Cam wasn't particularly keen on. I remember the empowerment I felt, being able to buy that home all by myself. It was an important marker for me that I didn't *need* a husband or a man or anyone else; I was completely self-sufficient—and then some. I'd worked my ass off all of my life. I deserved this, and it felt damn good.

Standing at the top of the stairs of my three-story tree house, we had our first kiss.

It felt *different. He* felt different.

After that first night, Adrian and I were together constantly. All that chivalry I'd craved seemed to be offered up on a silver platter all at once. I couldn't believe it. I felt like I had manifested this man. It felt too good to be true.

He was exactly the person I had been looking for. He was happy for me and everything I'd built. He saw me for who I was and knew how to support me where I needed to be supported.

It felt like a fairy tale—but like all fairy tales, there were some monsters to slay.

Lessons I've Learned

Starting Over Is a Necessity

I think the phrase "starting over" freaks people out. Like something bad happened. But sometimes it represents a rebirth of sorts, which is damn good news.

I'll never forget someone telling me the story of the lotus flower when I was trying to find my footing as a single mom whose life got thrown upside down. If you haven't heard about the lotus flower, allow me to enlighten you.

Back in Egyptian times, the lotus flower was very important in their religion. It was a symbol of the sun, of creation and birth, because at nightfall, the lotus closes and goes beneath the water, and at dawn, it climbs up above the water and reopens.

Lotuses root themselves in the mud, their lengthy stems

reaching upward to find the top of the water. There, the lush blossoms grow, and as the lotus blooms, the blossoms unfold one by one. Petal by petal, each one emerges pristine from the mucky water thanks to a repellent, protective outer coating. These day-blooming plants submerge and close at night, only to reawaken above the water every morning. The petals last for just a handful of days before shedding.

Let that settle in. Isn't it wonderful to think about this metaphor for life? It's only through the darkness that we find the light (someone said that way before me, obviously). But it's so damn true. While it feels nearly impossible when you're facedown in the dirt to imagine anything else, it's the actual grime and shit we sludge through that ends up reflecting the light.

Think about it: most greatness is born from frustration or something we don't like, something we want to change.

When we need something, big or small, the best ideas (and businesses!) come from a place of need, desire, and deep longing.

So what's the takeaway?

- Don't fucking sweat it. It will work out the way it's supposed to.
- Don't let failing get you down.
- Don't worry if people look at you sideways when you tell them about your idea.
- Don't let that bad call get you down; there's a better one for you right around the corner.

We all spend a lot—I repeat, *a lot*—of extra time worrying about shit we can't control. PSA: you know we *can* control very, very little in our lives, right? So stop trying!

My best advice that has served me very well is to keep chasing your happiness. And regularly ask yourself: Are you happy? Happy at your work? In your marriage? With your friendships and relationships?

If you answered no to any of those, then get cracking. Life is full of opportunities when you are willing to see them, but they aren't ever (*ever*) going to fall into your lap. You have to work for them (like, really hard). Set your mind and intentions on what you want (or what you think you want) and see what happens.

Come on—I dare you.

We All Have Baggage: Put It in the Attic

If you're a human (and I'm assuming you are if you're reading this), you have baggage. There's no avoiding it.

It doesn't matter if you've never been married or don't have kids; *everyone* has baggage. We all seem to have this awful habit of vomiting out old stories to new partners, creating this picture of who we are because of who we've loved and where we've been before. I think the healthiest way to look at our history is that we know it's in the past; we're not carrying it around with us like luggage. If someone wants to hear about it or see it, then we can put it on display, but we never have to leave it there.

We bring our expectations and our disappointments, our stereotypes and our dreams, into new relationships or new ventures. So we never really have a clean slate, and that's okay.

When you are starting over (and you've been hurt and disappointed), can you really go into the relationship with a clean slate? Can you forget about all the annoying habits your ex had? Can you drop your fears of being hurt again? Can you truly look at the person across from you with fresh eyes, giving them the benefit of the doubt?

If you've never done it before, it's worth it. It's worth it to start over, to wipe away the old, smeared residue of the past and step fully into the present.

When you start something new, you get to *be* new. You don't have to be selfish or loud or messy. You can re-create who you want to be in this relationship now. You can shuck off those old traits and focus on loving who you are and the one you're with, while you can.

Doesn't that sound more fun than waiting for the other shoe to drop?

Love Yourself First

If I've learned one thing as a woman in my forties, it's this: *no man will ever love you enough—you have to love yourself.*

I spent so much of my twentysomething years searching for love. I thought if I had the right man, then I could get married. If I could get married, then I could have babies. And if I had babies, then I'd have a purpose and be happy! The same went with business and success. As I climbed the proverbial ladder to success, I was always searching outside of myself to fill the void of loving who I was, *as* I was: without a man or business or living in a fancy city or a huge house.

What we all want, but what we so often don't see, is love from ourselves. You cannot enter a healthy relationship with someone else without loving who *you* are *now*—the messes, the mistakes, the hurts, the fears—as well as who you've been.

Whenever I tried to look outside of myself for validation, it was short-lived. Now I know that Adrian can't *make* me a good person. He can't *make* me more valuable or lovable. I will never be *more* of anything because of him.

This was a critical distinction for me the second time around, because I was no longer looking for love to make me feel better. Only *I* can make myself feel better.

There's such a difference.

Do I forget this and fall back into my old type of behavior sometimes? Of course. But then I continue to do the work of loving myself. Are you using your relationships (or work) to make yourself feel better? If so, start to untangle yourself from those sticky webs and do the real work of loving yourself *first*.

You love yourself first so that you're not using other people to fill the gaps you can't fill. If you love yourself first, then you're more apt not to be focusing on yourself all day trying to get your needs met. Other people show up on your radar.

Part of loving yourself is breaking that self-obsession.

The *real* love story
in life is the one you
create with yourself.

What is one thing you've never told anyone?

Chapter Ten

Your Great Big Idea Is Usually Your Next One

Don't be afraid to let go of what was in
order to discover what's next.

Though Drybar was an epic success, looking back, I realize there were things I could have done differently (hello, obsessive micromanager!).

While I have zero regret and I learned a shit ton about business, I also learned a ton more about myself and how to be a better leader, better spouse, better mother, better friend, and ultimately the best version of me.

I firmly believe that all the lessons from my Drybar days (many of which I learned the hard way) taught me something I finally became willing to see. As I reflect back on the last thirteen years (since we launched Drybar)—and my entire life, for that matter—self-awareness is what constantly rolls around in my head. It's incredibly important to be self-aware of the pain or discomfort you are causing others.

There are few things more powerful than self-awareness. Please go get some if you don't already have it! I can't emphasize this enough. If you get nothing else out of this book, please take away this one most important nugget. Being aware of your shortcomings, the areas you struggle with, or the things that everyone *else* sees is the biggest gift you can give yourself.

Once we sold the business, I pretty quickly realized that my identity, while tied up in Drybar for so many years, was about to significantly change. Who the hell was I now without this mammoth business to guide me?

Yes, I had a new relationship with Adrian, but even that hit a few rocky patches. When the pandemic hit, Adrian and I had only been together five months, but we made the leap and moved in together. We also knew, however, that it was make-or-break for us.

Up until that point, my time with Adrian had been *ours*. When we were together, it had been just us. Now, we were suddenly shacking up in my bachelorette pad half the time with his kiddos (then three and five) in The Hills, and I began to feel emotionally and physically claustrophobic.

While it was easy to fall in love with Adrian, dating him also meant mothering someone else's children and having a relationship with his ex-wife for the foreseeable future. I'd forgotten what it was like having little kids around. I didn't know what I could and couldn't say or do, or how much to involve myself. It was all pretty new and uncomfortable.

It was a lot to wrap my head around. At the beginning, every single time he picked up a call or text from his ex, my body would tense, and it had *nothing* to do with her. It could've been anyone. It just was a necessary and unavoidable violation of what we perceive as a natural rule: *don't talk to an ex.*

Ironically, I would talk to Cam on a semiregular basis. That seemed natural and justified. I hadn't yet done the work on growing my own self-awareness, so I was blind to my hypocrisy. Seeing, knowing, and eventually befriending your own fears is a *huge* part of the self-awareness I'm referring to.

It was a struggle to be parents and romantic partners when

Adrian and I were still getting to know each other. It was a struggle to figure out how to make our worlds seamlessly fit.

It led to lots of fights and conversations. I was simultaneously falling in love and also navigating mothering someone else's children.

Plus, with *all* the kids home all day every day, life was a pressure cooker, a constant litmus test for what I could handle and what I couldn't—or at least that was the conversation I was having in my own head about it. My definition of myself and my willingness to evolve for the sake of love would be the biggest challenge of this relationship. It was an endless stream of judgment calls, and every moment felt like high stakes. I wasn't sure when to step in and when to give the kids space, and I could never gauge when to work myself into systems that were already in place between Adrian and the kids. During that time, we had some tough conversations about whether I was up for the challenge of being the new stepmom, and it was really the only question mark in our relationship.

Could I hack it?

The complications of our messy life challenged us. It took me a long time to get to the point of being able to say, "Yes, I can do this," because I wasn't just starting a family or falling in love or getting a divorce; I was trying to master a million relationship skills at once.

Every day was like walking across a minefield. Every conflict was tedious, every phone call with our exes left everyone tense, and every interaction with Adrian's children required so much intention and thought that by the end of the day, I was totally exhausted.

But every night I fell into bed with Adrian, and I somehow knew it was all worth it. I *wanted* this life. I *wanted* to be there with him.

It was worth the mess.

. . . .

At the time, we'd officially sold Drybar. But one of the things no one ever talks about is that once you sell, you are no longer the mother to that "baby" you grew. You have no say in how the business runs, in the quality, customer service, nothing; it is no longer your problem to solve.

You walk away with cash, but you also just walk away—which, in my experience, was a mixed bag of emotions. In some ways, there was an awesome relief and freedom. A lot of freedom to do whatever I wanted, to pursue new passions, to start new businesses, to take more vacations, spend more time at home, and so on. There were many, many payoffs. But it also came with a lot of reflection on self-worth and feeling irrelevant.

I struggled (still do) quite a bit figuring out who I was without Drybar being my main focus, day in and day out. There was also a part of my passion that was a great distraction from the other aspects of life I had been justified in keeping lower in priority.

When that "big game" goes away, there is a "holy shit" moment of dealing with the other aspects of life. Kinda like the difference between a Friendsgiving and a traditional family Thanksgiving. Friendsgiving is 100 percent your choice of who you invite. But family Thanksgiving is a mixed bag. You love them all, but you're closer to some family members and have a distant or nonexistent relationship with others. (Let me just pause here and say: this is not a pity party, and I fully realize how damn lucky I am. I'm not, for one second, looking for sympathy.)

I am simply sharing what my personal journey looked like as I built and sold a company. I want to be very sensitive to anyone reading this, especially those of you may be rolling your eyes and thinking, *Oh yeah, you must have it real rough*. I don't. I'm extremely blessed and lucky and even more grateful to be where I am. But that's not the end of my story.

Quite frankly, witnessing the evolution of Drybar over the last few years has been a bit hard to stomach.

It was difficult to see the brand I poured my heart and soul into end up in new hands that didn't seem to care for or nurture it quite the way we did.

Alas, life is too short for hard feelings. When you sell your business, you turn over the keys to the kingdom. Every founder's story is different. Some founders stay more involved than others. I was never asked to stay involved, which I think—well, who am I kidding, I *know*—was a massive blow to my ego. I wasn't needed anymore, and that hurt. But life goes on, and things change and evolve.

. . . .

Someone once asked me if I had spiritually made peace with parting ways with Drybar. My quick response was, "Yes, totally." But I spent the next few months pondering that question. *Had I?* Probably not.

While a piece of my heart will always belong to Drybar, I am ready and excited for the next chapter. Speaking of new chapters, after Adrian and I got married (spoiler alert for the next chapter!), I realized I was entering uncharted waters. Once we returned from our honeymoon, we settled back into life at home, with Adrian rapidly expanding his leadership consulting company, as I continued to pave my new way.

In the last few years of Drybar, my brother was itching to start a massage concept, because he was frustrated with the very bleak massage landscape. Pre-Drybar, blowouts were not nearly as popular as they are today. We also really thought we could improve the massage world and desperately wanted to find a way. However, we were still busy with Drybar, so we approached Brittany Driscoll, who had been running marketing at Drybar for several years (and totally kicking ass). Brittany decided to leap in with us, and Squeeze was born. It's been an exciting journey to build another beloved brand, but this time as an adviser and investor, not in the day-to-day grind. It felt like quite the honor to be able to help another woman enter the CEO/cofounder role. Brittany completely blew us away in the Drybar era and has soared to an incredible leader at Squeeze. When you find someone like Brittany, hold on tight. They are rare.

Part of the reason Drybar worked so well was because nothing like it existed. Sure, blowouts had been around forever, but we created a beautiful, inviting space with an approachable price point *plus* world-class branding (thanks, Cam!). Quite simply, Drybar filled a hole in the marketplace.

We felt this same pain in the massage space. Enter Squeeze, a way better massage experience. Part of what makes Squeeze so unique is the technology we created. While it's a brick-and-mortar business where you physically go in for a massage, you book, pay, and tip all through our customized app. Not only that, as you go through the booking process, you choose *all* your preferences, from the type of pressure you like to the room temp, oil or lotion, and on and on. Just like Drybar, we thought about all the things we felt were missing from existing massage concepts and incorporated all those special details into the Squeeze experience. I'm proud to report that by the time this book comes out, we will have franchised close to seventy-five locations. Yes, Squeeze is a completely franchised model.

Now, as a proud investor, adviser, and cofounder of Squeeze, Okay Humans (the future of face-to-face talk therapy), and Brightside (an infrared yoga and sauna studio), I am not in the weeds like I was in the early Drybar days. I've had the freedom to explore new things, new roles, and new experiences. To date, I sit on the board of the largest medical spa in the United States, Ideal Image, and I serve as an adviser to Glowbar, a kick-ass thirty-minute expert facial concept, as well as The Bardot, a wedding day onsite beauty bus concept.

I've also taken on an exciting new role as the president of Canopy. The founders of Canopy reimagined the humidifier and made it look chic rather than medical. Humidifier, you ask? *Yes.* Trust me when I say it is the best beauty hack out there. Who knew? (Not me!) It has been such a cool and different experience to join a fully formed, yet still at heart a start-up operation—one that has already had tremendous success and growth in one short year.

This is a new phase in life, and I feel relieved to find a new professional purpose, which means not growing something of my own from the ground up, but helping other founders grow and nurture *their* businesses.

Speaking of helping other founders grow and following their passions, I love, love, love jewelry, so I've also teamed up with my now dear friend Meredith Quill to help her take her small jewelry company to the next level. Together we formed Becket and Quill. Our collection is made up of gorgeous, intentional pieces that are high *end* but not high *spend*. The direct-to-consumer (DTC) world was new to me, and frankly, I didn't know what I was doing. I've made a lot of mistakes over the years while learning this new business, but I love taking on new adventures and stretching myself. Turns out, despite being a shitty student back in the day, I really do love learning about things I love. Go figure.

I have come to realize and appreciate that through our work, we are *always* seeking purpose. We're forever reinventing ourselves to keep evolving and not allowing life to get stale or boring. Don't ignore that little voice inside begging you to make a change. I wholeheartedly believe in this mantra and have continued to try new things outside my typical skill set, like taking on all these new roles.

It can feel scary to take risks and try new opportunities, and to let go of all that you've built in the pursuit of something new or unfamiliar. But taking risks is where the good stuff is. Whether you want to grow something from the ground up or not, there is so much you learn through each phase of business.

So take the risk. Take a leap of faith. Try something new.

I know I am, and I'll never stop.

Lessons I've Learned

When You Build Something New, Understand You're Leaving Something Behind

Letting go is hard.

Whether you are letting go of a relationship, a business, or a friendship, or when a child is leaving the nest, change can seem like the worst thing on earth.

As a business owner, selling your company, folding, or walking away can sometimes feel like a betrayal. Your business has become this *thing* you've birthed and nurtured. How can any price tag make letting go of that okay?

Most of us know when it's time to pivot. We can feel that

crackle of energy beneath the surface with our next big idea. But when you step into that new thing, you can't bring the old thing with you. You can't bring the old business to the new business. You can't bring the old relationship into a new relationship.

You are leaving a piece of yourself behind (and maybe it's a piece that needs to be left). You are leaving a bit of yourself—your passion, your mistakes, your triumphs—either for someone else to capitalize on or for everyone to forget.

Moving on is hard, but it is necessary for growth. Make sure, when you move on, that you are really ready to say goodbye, to sever those ties. Create a ritual. Journal about it. Pick a friend to share every piece of the struggle with. Have an event. Celebrate the end, just as you would the beginning. You need to have closure, no matter what. If it's not given to you, create it. This closure will help you as you move on to other things.

If You Love the Team You Built, Take Them With You When You Go

One of the coolest things about growing a business is that you get to build your own team.

Sometimes you find a unicorn; sometimes you find a dud. But usually, if you run a business long enough, you find your heroes, the people you would take with you to the edge of the world. We had so many amazing employees at Drybar, people I wasn't ready to part with.

The beauty of building your own brand is that you are also investing in people. Being able to recognize your strengths and weaknesses is—and I know I've said this before, but it bears repeating—an absolutely necessary strength.

While there will be many things you have to learn along the way, recognizing what you aren't good at and bringing other people in to help is a recipe for success. This was a hard one for me to learn. I wanted to do everything myself. I wanted to make all the decisions and do all the things all the time. (Well, okay, not payroll. I really sucked at that.)

But I'm here to tell you, there is not only greater freedom as you bring in more qualified people, but it will also help your business so much.

I am huge on loyalty and trust; the people who are in the trenches with you before the business is a success are usually the ones to trust. I have been so lucky in my career to have so many people I want to continue to work with.

Keep this in mind when building your team. Make sure you are bringing in people you want to be by your side no matter what, even if they don't have the best résumé you've ever seen. Always hire from the heart.

Follow Your Passion, Even If It Feels Ridiculous

Along my journey, I've learned that I can't get far if I don't lead with passion.

With Drybar, I stuck to my roots (literally) and built something based around a true love of mine: hair. I turned to what I loved, what I was passionate about, and what I could see doing for a long time.

When you are thinking about building something new, consider your passions, even if they feel like a hobby or something you think people wouldn't take seriously. What do you love to do? What doesn't feel like work to you? What can you lose yourself in completely? Are you stuck in a job you dread, or are you working for someone you don't really respect? Are you itching to do something for yourself and dying to pursue your *real* dream?

I have met a lot of wannabe entrepreneurs who don't ever take that leap because they don't feel ready. Sound familiar? Guess what? *No one is ever ready*. Read that again. Some may *think* they are ready, but I promise you, you would be hard-pressed to find one founder who would tell you, "Yup, I had all the answers and knew exactly what I was doing." I can barely even write that sentence because it's just so ridiculously false. Moreover, anyone who's thought that is probably on their third business idea that has crashed and burned. Dogma is the end of an entrepreneur.

Starting your own business is hard and complicated and certainly not for everyone, but if there is a burning idea or a thing you wish was better, I urge you to consider giving it a go. It may not work, and you could fail, but you will never know what could have been if you don't even try.

Post-Drybar, my purpose has shifted a lot. Now, to be able to help other entrepreneurs learn what I've learned over the last thirteen years, and to be able to share that knowledge with the next generation of leaders, really thrills me. It fills me up and makes me feel like I'm exactly where I am supposed to be.

Are you exactly where you are supposed to be? What fills you up? What are you longing to pour your time and energy into?

Whatever the answer, follow that road, even if it takes you far from where you are now.

Spend time doing what you love; *outsource* the rest.

How can you use your mess to embrace exactly who you are?

Chapter Eleven

You're Going to Be Fine . . . Mostly

The magic of new beginnings is that anything is possible.

I stood inside my gorgeous bridal suite at The Landsby hotel in Solvang, California, staring at my bouquet of delicate garden roses in varying hues of mauve, compliments of Creative Light Design, that matched my custom-made pink dress, compliments of Emily Current and Meritt Elliot, the brilliantly talented designers and founders of The Great.

Here I was, about to walk down the aisle for the second and final time. I was going to become a wife again, with all my friends and family in attendance.

I took a deep breath. Adrian and I had taken over the entire hotel so that we could drape it in our own flowers, photos, music, and overall ambiance, with all fifty-two rooms reserved for our nearest and dearest.

On the other side of where I stood, 130 guests waited for me as "What a Wonderful World" by Louis Armstrong played. I walked arm-in-arm with my father down the veranda that overlooked our beautiful community of friends and family, then into the courtyard that led down the steps where my beloved boys were waiting to meet me and walk me to Adrian. The only thing missing was my mom.

Over the course of our relationship, my boys had completely

fallen in love with Adrian too. It has been one of the greatest joys of my life to witness the beautiful bond that formed between them. Adrian never tried to replace their father; rather, he just wanted to be their friend and has become a man they love, admire, and constantly learn from.

When I looked around, I simply thought, *Look what love does. Look what love can do.* I felt so happy, so content at where my life was headed and couldn't wait to be Adrian's wife.

This was a huge moment. After a whirlwind romance where Adrian and I worked through so much—like learning how to love better and put down our dukes (as he likes to say), stop trying to be right all the time, and figure out how to blend our unique families, all while under COVID lockdown—we had finally made it. We knew what we wanted. We knew what our relationship meant. And we were about to celebrate it publicly.

My heart fluttered and my hands shook as I glanced over at my bridesmaids and best friends, all looking stunning dressed in ivory, gathered by the flower altar (huge shout-out to Creative Light). It was like our own secret garden, spilling with the most breathtaking pink and peach flowers. Everything was simply perfect.

It felt like I was wading through an English garden full of spring flowers to get to my groom. As the boys hugged Adrian, I stepped toward him, practically exploding with excitement and the anticipation of becoming his wife. Emotion brimmed in his eyes when he saw me.

Throughout the entire ceremony, Adrian was completely locked into me, even though I kept looking around, smiling and waving to everyone in attendance. I felt such a sense of love and warmth to be surrounded by the people I loved most in the world. We were both nervous as we read our own vows in front of friends and family. I stared down at our wrists, where we'd each had a line from our vows tattooed.

No matter what.

After it was official, we were welcomed into the reception as Mr. and Mrs. for the first time. Flower boxes adorned the courtyard, mixed with natural greenery. The farm tables were accented with ceramic bud vases bursting with pink flowers that matched my dress and gorgeous chairs.

We slow-danced, forehead to forehead, to "North" by Sleeping at Last, which is a song that carries deep meaning for Adrian of a time when his life was in pieces, and he felt very alone and uncertain of his future. He played it for me early on, and it became ours.

I stared into Adrian's eyes, delighting in the fact that, after everything, we had made it. We were here. *Married!*

At dinner, we feasted on crab cakes, racks of lamb, pan-seared salmon, and locally sourced vegetables, and we rounded it out with a delicate two-tier red velvet cake, outfitted in fresh blooms to continue the garden theme.

Adrian and I lost ourselves on the dance floor, our kids in tow. "Hooked on a Feeling" came on as our first official family dance, and we were huddled together and so damn excited to be there. We brought down the house. It felt like a declaration of our collective love and commitment between the six of us. It was quite a sight as we all jumped and smiled, reveling in our celebration until the dance floor emptied out and we flocked to the makeshift karaoke portion of the night where Adrian serenaded me with "She's Some Kind of Wonderful." Yes, it was amazing. Yes, Adrian is a phenomenal singer. And yes, I am completely smitten with this man. Around 2 a.m., exhausted and exhilarated, we stumbled back to our suite, and the glorious night came to an end.

It felt like the beginning of something, and the end of something else. A chance to begin again, to reclaim a part of myself, and to step into an entirely new chapter. A chapter of my life that has brought me here, to you.

. . . .

Here we are.

When I first sat down to write this book, I wasn't exactly sure what I wanted the takeaway to be. Did I want to teach you about business? Did I want to inspire you? Did I want to show you the underbelly of my life, with all its missteps and messes and beautiful mistakes?

The answer is yes. Yes to it all. I wanted to show you all of me, because for so many of us, what we see online or onstage really amounts to not much more than that godforsaken highlight reel. And that's not real. Success isn't won through the highlights. That's not where the good stuff is anyway. The good stuff is *here*, in the middle and the mess.

Personal transformation happens in the deep and vulnerable transitions in life: the divorce, the roller-coaster business, the loss of a boy to rehab, the loss of my mother, the loss of myself. It was in finding myself again, finding love again, finding my son again—and finding that I'm both *in* and *above* all of this mess in the middle. It's in all these places that I've found myself again, that I've reclaimed who I am beyond being the creator of Drybar.

It's been here, on these pages, that I've been able to look at the whole picture of my life and take a deep breath. I've won some, and I've lost some, but I'm here to talk about it, to embrace it all. It has been a cathartic and vulnerable journey sharing everything here with you, but it's also been a privilege, and I sincerely hope it inspires you in some small way.

I want you to know that no matter what your goal, no matter what you want to pursue both personally and professionally, it's worth it. *You're* worth it. Going after what we want in life is what fills us with meaning, joy, and tenacity. I believe in you. I believe that if you have audacious willingness, grit, and humility, the sky is just the starting point, not the limit.

Please have the guts to go find out what you're made of and how far you can soar. Then, when you find your limits, experiment, ask for help, and take a good hard look in the mirror and understand that you are capable of more than you are currently willing to believe.

You really do create your own reality, and whether you're an entrepreneur, an aspiring entrepreneur, a stay-at-home parent, an employee, a divorcé, or you're curled in a ball, not knowing what to do next, it's good to understand that *we are all in the same boat.*

We are all searching. We all want success and happiness. We all want to feel okay. No matter where you are on the journey, here's the *real* messy truth: Everything changes. Nothing will be good or bad forever. Life always ebbs and flows. Some days are great, and some days are terrible. It's only when we learn to embrace all of it—the good, the bad, and the messy—that we start to learn that the in-between is where we create resilience, where we begin to tell the *real* story, and where we open ourselves up to share who we really are.

Though this book has been all about my life, my sincere hope is that you walk away motivated and empowered to embrace your own mess.

Because I can tell you, the best parts are most certainly the messy parts—the shit that seems impossible to figure out and navigate. And while we can't always comprehend why something didn't turn out quite the way we wanted it to, I assure you it all works out the way it's supposed to in the end. Instead of regrets, focus on learning and moving forward.

Lessons I've Learned

Be Kind

This is the holy grail, the very key to success on all levels of life, both in business and on a personal level. It is *truly* one of the most important lessons of all. Though you won't always *want* to be kind and there will be days when it feels like it's all falling apart and everything is wrong and everyone is driving you nuts, *those* are the days and the moments when you must dig deep to show kindness. I believe this is a lifelong practice and one we all fail at sometimes, so let this serve as a reminder to be kind to yourself and others. As my father always says, "You catch more flies with honey than with vinegar."

What Do You Really Love?

Plato once said that "our need will be the real creator."[9] So when thinking of your next great idea, a good place to start is to ask yourself: *What is something I really love or want to love that doesn't quite yet exist?* Reinvention or improving something that *does* actually exist into something way better (like we did with blowouts at Drybar, massages at Squeeze, and humidifiers with Canopy) is also a great place to start. Chances are, someone else feels the exact same way you do and would want to buy or use your product or service.

You Don't Have to Go to Every Argument You're Invited To

These wise words are an Adrian special. I wish I had learned this little nugget of wisdom much, much earlier in my career. Not everything has to be a battle. You don't have to go to the mat over every single situation that arises. Sometimes the smarter, better, and more productive thing to do is walk away. (Remember my number one takeaway, be kind? This is where it matters!) Take a deep breath, and don't send that insidious email or text (ugh, *guilty*). Instead, learn to just let some things go.

Find People Smarter and More Experienced Than You to Help Build Your Dream Business

You can't do it all yourself (I learned that the hard way). You need other people's perspectives, experience, and wisdom to keep your business alive and thriving. I see a lot of entrepreneurs wanting to hold all the cards (and equity) and do everything themselves. Sorry to be the bearer of bad news, but chances are you aren't great at everything. I know I certainly wasn't. And that's okay. Find those key people to fill in the gaps, the areas you aren't great in. Hiring good people is *just* as important as the business itself. You are only as strong as your team.

Focus on the Details

You also don't have to create the next iPhone, but you do have to nail the details. There doesn't have to be a complete white space in order for your idea to exist. When we started Drybar, we reinvented something that already existed: blowouts. We just created a much better experience around *getting* a blowout. We created a brand around it and made it a top-notch experience, from the customer service to the decor to the millions of little details people really do care about, whether they know it or not. Branding is much more than just a great logo and a tagline. It's all those small details that encompass an extraordinary overall experience. For example, are you paying attention to fresh flowers that don't have dirty water, a super clean space, incredibly kind staff, clear messaging or signage, and a clear flow of operation? Even if you aren't the next Steve Jobs (and who knows, you might be!), whatever you create needs to focus on the details, because they matter the most.

You Are Probably the Last Person to Know That You Are Sometimes the Problem

This one is a doozy, guys. And oh man, this is also a newer lesson for me. Sometimes, it takes me a while to realize—wait for it—that *I am the actual problem*. I am the issue. It's me, hi. This can show up in many ways. My best advice is to work on your self-awareness and to talk to those closest to you personally and professionally; you know those people in your life who will give it to you straight. No sugarcoating, please. Honesty makes us all better.

Stick to What You Know, and Keep It Simple

When we started Drybar, I knew how to give a mean blowout. I'd spent years and years on my craft (Malcom Gladwell's ten-thousand-hours rule[10] tends to make you an expert), and I knew hair really well. Because of my dedication and passion for hair and blowouts, I felt very strongly about keeping the focus on what I knew in my bones and knew I could be successful at. When investors wanted us to consider doing manicures or sell makeup to the women who were consistently, week after week, coming to Drybar, it simply didn't feel right to me, despite the fact that we definitely *could* have made a lot of money doing those things. I stuck to my gut and wanted to focus on this one thing and be the absolute best at it. Getting compared to In-N-Out Burger was and still is one of the greatest compliments I ever received. (They could easily sell you a chicken sandwich, but they don't, and that's why they have the best burgers and fries around.) Stick to what you know, folks. And keep it simple.

Being an Entrepreneur Is Hard Work

During my time as an entrepreneur, I've learned that this isn't a thing you do; it's a muscle you flex. Being an entrepreneur takes *a lot*. It's incredibly hard work, often thankless work, even, and the payoff usually takes much longer than expected or desired.

There are certain people who are built for it, and others who don't have that same fire or risk tolerance. That said, you may grow into being an entrepreneur and get to the point where you just *have* to do this thing on your own and are no longer interested in building someone else's empire. I have seen it happen time and time again. You can always reinvent yourself—*always*.

Accept Progress Over Perfection

Another invaluable lesson I learned was to accept progress over perfection. (This is a lesson I learned from my brother.) I used to get really stuck in the proverbial weeds and felt like things had to be just so to move forward. Turns out, they don't. It even pains me to type this, but things can be rocky and messy and not at all figured out in the beginning and you can still go, start, launch. Wherever you are, know that everything has the ability to improve over time. All things do.

It's Okay to Not Have All the Answers

Lastly, it's okay to not have all the answers. Even if you don't know the answers, start anyway. Nothing good ever comes from a comfort zone.

A Final Word

Despite all these tips, even now, I still have to remember my own advice. I struggle to keep the balance because I love to overwork. I don't meditate enough. I don't always get it right, but I've realized that to live the best life I can, all of it goes back to one little word: purpose. Purpose in my daily life, in my relationships, in my professional endeavors, and with my kids.

So, I ask: What's your purpose? What's it all about *for you*? How do you want to show up in this great big world? Are you afraid of the mess, or are you ready to lean into it? Regardless of your answer, it's your time to dig in, to expand, and to explore who you really are and what you're made of.

This is your one big, beautiful, messy life.

How do you want to spend it?

The takeaway is simple: Embrace who you are, right now. Take a deep breath, and dive in. Find your messy truth and own that shit.

I'm rooting for you.

What do you want to do next?

Afterword

I've been dreading adding this, but I feel I owe it to all of you to be as truthful and as transparent as possible.

So here goes.

On May 17, 2023, Adrian and I separated. The simple reason is that we both wanted something that never came to be.

To protect our children, I am going to keep the rest private. But here is what I will share. . .

As you may have noticed in this book, my self-worth has largely been entangled with many things: romantic partners, businesses, outside validation. I've done a lot of outsourcing instead of self-sourcing, and I am coming to realize that I have relied on other people and things to make me happy for far too long. First, it was Cam. Then my boys—then my business—then Adrian.

I am slowly and painfully realizing that no one else can make me happy. Not my husband. Not my kids. Not my success. Not my readers. Not my friends.

It's me.

Since the day Adrian and I separated, I have been in deep pain and darkness. A grief I have never experienced has washed over me and taken me down so deep. I am desperately trying to catch my breath.

I won't sugarcoat it. It has been hell, but I am also very, very grateful for the myriad gifts this break has shown me. It has revealed so much work that I need to do on myself. I am not proud of how I always showed up in my marriage, and I intend to dig in and find out why—on my own, one day at a time. My patterns, my past traumas, my abandonment issues, and child-hood wounds are fascinating and so revealing—and I've only just begun to scratch the surface.

With all my heart, I wish I had done this work earlier and taken more responsibility for my actions, but rarely do we humans really sink our teeth into this work until tragedy arrives at our door, kicking it open with unexpected force. I am deeply grateful to my father who has helped me see things in my upbringing that I now realize have contributed to my relationship with men.

Yes, I'm heartbroken and I wish things were different. Losing part of my family has felt like hitting rock bottom; however, it has also launched me into important work that I have needed to do for quite some time.

This isn't easy work; just like the title of this book, it's messy and uncomfortable, and I'm realizing there is no "happily ever after." Being okay is part of doing the work: the work of eradicat-ing my past traumas, shifting my own energy and mindset, and getting myself to a healthier place, regardless of what is going on around me. It's going to be a long road, but I will get there, step by step.

Even though Adrian and I are separated, this book is still the truth of my life during these years. Nothing about my journey discounts the happiness, the growth, or the memories of our time together. This is a long life of learning, and I'm grateful for these chapters that encapsulate some formative years of that journey. Take what you will from it; I pray it gives you an expansive horizon to look upon and endless hope for your own messy truth.

I have worked so hard on this beautiful book, and wish I was able to end it on a happier note, but if life has taught me anything, it's this:

Everything changes.
Life shows us what we need to learn and when we need to learn it.
Every season is an opportunity to learn and grow.
Don't ever get too comfortable or complacent.
Keep your heart wide open to love.
Stay curious.
Let shit go.
Enjoy every moment.
Love yourself, even when you don't.

And *that* is the Messy Truth.

Acknowledgements

To my mama, Rozi, wherever you are. For teaching me about beauty and giving me the confidence to become the best version of myself. I miss you every day.

To my dad, Phil, for making me the strong woman I am today. And for teaching me so many life-changing lessons. I'm so proud to be your daughter.

To my brother, forever business partner, and first best friend, Michael. For believing in me since day one. Since we were kids, you have always taken care of me in the most beautiful way. Thank you for changing my life. Beyond grateful for you.

To my best friend, Paige, for years of countless talks and tears. Our friendship is one of my life's greatest joys.

To Lauren Gallo, Sara Happ, Sarah Gibson Tuttle; your support and love are everything to me.

To Rea Frey Holguin, for championing my voice and your unending patience and enthusiasm while helping me craft my story in the most authentic way.

To Sloane Cavitt Logue, for your unwavering confidence in me and for pushing me to tell the world my story, my way.

To Jeff Williams, for your endless support both legally and emotionally.

To Brittany Driscoll, for your brilliant mind and hardworking spirit. Love building and growing with you. Our hard-earned friendship means the world to me.

To Cameron Webb, for giving me the two most wonderful boys and so much more. While our story took an unexpected turn, I'm forever grateful for our partnership.

To the Drybar stylists, managers, bartenders, and leaders who took a leap of faith with me and worked their asses off to make this little yellow dream a reality.

To John Heffner, Janet Gurwitch, Steve Berg, and Paul Pressler. Thank you for helping us build such an incredible company. Your guidance was priceless.

And finally, to the millions of badass, hardworking, forever-striving women who came to Drybar and supported our dream, your loyalty quite literally changed me. There really aren't enough words to adequately describe the depth of my gratitude. Thank you.

Notes

1. Mary Oliver, "Poem 133: The Summer Day," *New and Selected Poems* (Boston: Beacon Press, 1992).
2. The saying "Necessity is the mother of invention" is commonly attributed to Benjamin Jowett's popular translation (1871) of Plato's *Republic*, Book II, 369c: "The true creator is necessity, who is the mother of our invention." The literal translation is "Our need will be the real creator."
3. Alli Webb, *The Drybar Guide to Good Hair for All* (New York: Abrams Image, 2016), dedication.
4. Who remembers *Daily Candy*? It was a daily or weekly newsletter that was *the best* at breaking the coolest new thing and trend—pre-Instagram and social media as we know it today. If you got featured on DC, you were golden. Thanks, Crystal Meers!
5. "Just Keep Swimming," track 11 on *Finding Nemo: The Musical*, Walt Disney Records, 2007, CD.
6. No, I'm still not going to tell you his name.

7. Justice Louis D. Brandeis, *Other People's Money and How the Bankers Use It* (New York: Frederick A. Stokes, 1914), chapter 5, https://louisville.edu/law/library/special-collections/the-louis-d.-brandeis-collection/other-peoples-money-chapter-v.

8. Kenny Rogers, "The Gambler," written by Don Schlitz, track 1 on *The Gambler*, United Artists, 1978, album.

9. Plato, *Republic*, Book II, 369c.

10. Malcolm Gladwell, *Outliers: The Story of Success* (New York: Little, Brown, and Company, 2008), 39–42.

About the Author

Alli Webb is a *New York Times* bestselling author, business adviser, mentor, and co-founder of several businesses—most notably Drybar, which grew from one simple idea to hundreds of locations and a full hair care and styling product line, which she sold in 2019. She lives in Los Angeles.